The Surrender Paradox

After War, Disaster, and Betrayal, Is Surrender An Option?

CONTENTS

Can a Holy and Loving God take the pieces of a broken life and make the life whole again? What part does holiness play in the life of a broken Christian?

I have come to believe that God made each person with a unique, but finite ability to deal with the things that life throws at them, good or bad. Each person has a different capacity to deal with them and you do not get to choose what you are given. You can definitely work and improve that capacity, but you do not have a choice where you start. That is given to you and that is not the problem. The problem is what to do when you exceed your capacity.

Think of that capacity like the capacity of drinking glasses you use to get a glass of cool, refreshing water on a hot day. Some hold eight ounces. Some hold sixteen, some twenty, some thirty-two ounces. You do not get to choose how much water you can hold. You do not choose how much water gets poured into you. You only get a choice of what to do with the water that gets poured into you. You can choose how you respond to what happens to you. That is an incredibly important lesson I learned the hard way.

Normally, life pours relatively small amounts of water in, and you drink it (process it and deal with it), then it's gone and more is poured in and repeated.

INTRODUCTION

"Why would a loving God let something like this happen?"

"Why do such bad things happen to good people?"

These are just two of the extremely common questions so often asked through the tears of despair, loneliness and pain caused by the gut-wrenching trials of life. Sometimes they come as the result of a single, crisis event, like the sudden death of a child or a divorce, or other betrayal by a trusted friend. Other times, they come after a seemingly endless stream of smaller, yet still continuously draining negative events, like military deployments, being laid off a long held job, or physical illness.

But what do you do when big and smaller ones combine in a sustained attack that takes away seemingly everything a person holds dear? What if war and devastating natural disaster combine to knock you flat on your face and then you are kicked by those who should be helping you? What do you do if your cup of adversity overflows and you are completely broken?

ACKNOWLEDGEMENTS

If I did not have my own personal relationship with God, I would not be alive today. I am forever grateful to God for His love and grace that have sustained me through all my trials. I do not serve Him to get more love from Him. I serve Him because I love Him and am grateful for all He has already done. I also want to thank my incredible best friend and wife of eighteen years, Terri. You are my soul mate and gift from God! A lifetime is too short to show my love and gratitude for your love and support! For the multitude of times that I needed to tangibly feel God's presence and support, He sent me many men and women of God. Without the encouragement, help and support of my best friend of almost thirty five years, Reverend Nathan Buchanan, and my mentors and friends Chaplain Scott McChrystal, Chaplain Bill Coker, and Deacon Gene Garrison, my story would have turned out very different.

Sometimes life pours relatively small amounts of water in, and before you can drink it, more is poured in. You try to drink that, but more comes in. Before long, the level of water reaches the rim. If some is not drunk, the glass overflows. When it overflows, you are in a crisis.

Thankfully, less often, life pours large amounts of water in and overflows your cup quickly. You reach the crisis point suddenly.

Whether your cup overflowed through seemingly continuous pours of smaller amounts, or through a single large pour, the situation is the same. You are overflowing and in a crisis! What you do at those times could determine the course of your life. It did mine.

When you are overwhelmed with the overflow, surrender is the only way out. You cannot just fight your way out alone. But who or what you surrender to is of critical importance. Do you surrender control to the despair and hopelessness that seems to come from all directions, or do you surrender control to the God who created you and wants to sustain you and to give you life? Therein lies the Surrender Paradox. You MUST NOT surrender, but you MUST surrender.

This is the story of one man's answers to those questions and to the paradox, wrestled out in his own life. I am that man.

This is some of the story of my brokenness and my faith in God and His grace that brought me from being seconds from surrendering to despair and ending my life to the point of total surrender to God and being lifted up by Him and used to help others.

Some of my story is unique to me. Much of my story is like your story, too. By different means and in different measure the brokenness comes to us all. If you are struggling under the weight of despair or hopelessness, this book is for you. If you need encouragement that God really does care intimately about you, this book is for you. If you need to know that God can take broken pieces and make them into something that glorifies Him, this book is for you. I pray you will hear God speak all these and more to you through these pages of our shared story.

SURRENDER TO DESPAIR?

Sometimes you get hit by a blow that shatters you all at once.

Sometimes you get hit by many, smaller ones that fracture and shatter.

You usually don't get a choice.

Character cannot be developed in ease and quiet. Only through experience of trial and suffering can the soul be strengthened, ambition inspired, and success achieved.
Helen Keller

1

OF TACOS AND PANIC

January 2003 in Tucson, Arizona came to us with the joy of a new baby, born only five weeks before. As the war in Afghanistan raged on and there was talk of possible war with Iraq, possibilities of my deployment increased. In a freak accident the second week of January, I broke half a tooth while eating a "soft" taco. With a temporary fix in place, I waited for the permanent tooth to be made and implanted the following week. Then, the following week, the first deployment orders came.

My Wing Chaplain and mentor called me into his office and told me that I had orders to deploy three days later. He told me to go home and begin packing for a long deployment. I went home and told Terri. With a new baby in her arms, the news hit her hard. However, it was something we had known could happen and knew was a part of ministering to the military.

Two days later I was supposed to go to the dentist and have my tooth fixed. As I began preparations to deploy for months, I had no idea that I was the topic of discussion for several top base leaders. As part of preparing my orders, a review of my medical and dental readiness was performed. My broken tooth had made me temporarily non-deployable. However, it was to be fixed one day before I was to fly out. The discussion took about a day to come to a decision. My commander decided that the timetable was too close. If there were any complications with my tooth being fixed, I would hold up the whole troop movement while my replacement was readied. He removed me from the deployment and tasked one of my chaplain friends with it instead. He now had one day to prepare to deploy! I was relieved and also felt guilty for his only getting a very short notice.

Over the next six months, four more deployment orders came down to me, and three times they were cancelled. One was to a location I could tell my wife. One was to a location I could not tell my wife. One was to a location so classified that I would not be told where I was going until I was in the air, flying away from Tucson. Each time weighed heavier and heavier as I prepared, mentally and physically, and then had the deployment cancelled. Each time my cup got fuller.

After the fourth set of orders were cancelled, I decided that I needed to get away with my family and take a vacation to try to recuperate from the stress. Being close to the Mexican border, we decided to drive down to the Pacific coast of Mexico and vacation. While there, I decided to go SCUBA diving. I had been certified twelve years earlier in college, but hadn't dived since. I had just taken a refresher course and was looking forward to the excitement and beauty of diving. Little did I know just how "exciting" the dive would really turn out to be.

Dinner the day before my fateful dive…

The dive shop I went with took us out for the day on their boat, scheduling a couple dives before lunch and a couple after. There were only three of us diving that day, so I was paired with a married couple also on vacation. The three of us had great dives before lunch. We stopped for lunch onboard. We had fresh fish tacos! They tasted so good that I ate and ate. After a couple hour break, we went diving again. On that dive the three of us spread out farther. It was a fateful decision.

Only about twenty minutes into a sixty- minute dive, something happened to my air. At twenty-five feet below surface, I could not breathe! I felt as if someone was standing on my chest. I struggled for air, with panic quickly starting. As I inflated my Buoyancy Compensator (BC) and began a quick ascent to the surface, I remember telling myself, "John, if you panic, you will die! Keep control!" I struggled to remember my dive training. Without realizing it, in my haste to surface, I had over-inflated my BC and further constricted my breathing. I was on the razor's edge of panic when I reached the surface. I tore off my mask and gasped for air! Although I was at the surface, I still could not breathe! I then realized my over-inflation of my BC and let air out of it. I finally was able to breathe! As I looked around, I could not see the boat or my dive partners. I knew I would have to get out of the water as soon as I could. I saw a coral reef within swimming distance and struggled over and climbed its razor sharp edges. My wetsuit was being shredded, but at least I was out of the water.

When my dive partners lost sight of me, they surfaced and signaled to the boat. They got on board and began looking for me. They quickly found me on the reef and came as close as they safely could to me. To get in the boat I would have to swim over to it. Although most of the panic had subsided, almost everything in me was screaming, "Don't go back in the water!" Summoning what little courage I had left, I made the short swim to the boat. I sat on the boat as the other couple completed their final dive of the day. After that, we all headed back to the marina.

After talking with the dive master about what happened, it seemed likely that I had made a rookie mistake. I had eaten too much food and went diving too soon afterward. I felt so stupid! The tacos had almost killed me!

I told Terri about what happened, but downplayed the impact on me. I really did not yet know how much it had impacted me. My cup got much fuller…

2003/05/23

*The dive boat in the marina before we left…
If only I had known…*

2

THE ANXIETY BUILDS

Only weeks after getting back from my "vacation," I was sent to a conference on the East Coast. The day I was to fly home there was lots of bad weather across the country. Many flights were cancelled or delayed. One of my connecting flights was one of those cancelled. However, that was not a big deal to me. I would spend the night at a hotel and catch a flight back home the next morning. Since that would keep me from reporting back into my base for work the next morning, I knew I needed to inform my boss of the situation. I called him up and explained what was going on. He told me that was fine, but then said, "By the way, you've just got orders to go remote to Thule Greenland."

I felt as if a ton of bricks had just been dropped on me. Thule Air Base was in Greenland. A remote assignment would take me away from my family for one year. Although I knew remotes were possible, I had not even considered it might happen to me, especially with what I had been dealing with. But now I would have to do more than consider it. I would have to prepare and do it.

Dinner with my baby girl before getting news of me being away from her for a year in Greenland

I began the preparations for a permanent change of station (PCS) move to Greenland. Terri and I had to decide where she and the girls would live while I was gone. Although they could be permitted to stay in base housing while I was remote, we did not have any family in Tucson. We decided that Terri and the girls would move back to the Houston area, to be near family. There were so many details to work out, but we knew we were doing what God wanted us to do. That made it a bit easier.

Then history repeated itself.

One week before the packers were to arrive to pack my belongings and ship them to Greenland, my orders to move were cancelled. I was not going to go after all. Relief and frustration flooded over me. That was the fifth set of orders for me that had been cut off. My cup filled fuller.

Two short weeks passed until I was called into my Wing Chaplain's office again. As I stepped in his office, I said, "So where am I going Boss?" He said, "Balad, Iraq. Your (deployment) tasking has just come down. You will deploy in two weeks." I again prepared to deploy, half expecting that it would also be turned off. My cup filled fuller. As Terri and I walked into the airport for me to begin my deployment, I said to her, "I think this one is going to happen." I walked onto the plane and began a time that would forever change my life.

3

WAR: TO IRAQ AND BACK

After three exhausting days of traveling, on 27 October 2003, I arrived north of Baghdad, at Camp Anaconda. The US Army had taken what had been the Iraqi Air Force Academy six months earlier and had been holding it. The US Air Force was now coming in to repair the airfield and bring in large cargo planes of supplies and equipment. I was the first US Air Force chaplain to hit the ground there, as we built the airbase from the ground up. That night I was awakened from a deep sleep in the tent by a mouse walking on my chest. As I awoke with a start, I unknowingly launched the mouse into the air, either into orbit or onto one of the other fifteen guys sleeping around the tent! It was a little too much of a 'warm' welcome!

The next chaplain and the first chaplain assistant arrived the next day, along with the first mortar attack of my deployment. The third and final chaplain, also our Wing Chaplain, had a long travel delay that would keep him and his chaplain assistant from arriving for nearly ten days. Since I had slight seniority on the other chaplain, it fell to me to

14

lead our small team to establish the chapel and its programs on a bare base and have it running before the new Wing Chaplain arrived.

Warrior Servant?

John (dressed in his finest) helping make sand bags to protect tents from mortar and rocket blasts

Things went well and the chapel program was quickly meeting the religious needs of the growing base. As the days rolled into weeks, the spiritual and emotional needs of the men and women in uniform increased. Just about every person there was doing an incredible job of carving out an air base, but it took a toll on each one. As the only counselors on base, the three of us chaplains were always in demand. Often an Airman would step into my office and say "Chaplain, do you have a minute?" Most of the time, they would ask that as I was visiting them at work, on the flight line, in the fire station, Civil Engineering, or especially the Combat Army Surgical Hospital (CASH). Many were the times that I would walk towards the dining facility and have someone walk up next to me and say "Chaplain, do you have a minute?" I nearly always did, because they were the reason I was in Iraq. The conversation would turn to the news from back home about the sick baby, or the marriage problems, or the destruction and death that often visited the warzone we were serving in. Those were important discussions and opportunities for God to comfort and strengthen the men and women I was given the opportunity to care for. However, it also took a bit from my cup each time; some more than others, but always costing. Caring often hurts.

Several weeks into the deployment, I received an email from my parents telling me that they had just found out that a man from their church was working as a contractor at Camp Anaconda. His name was Dave Pressly. My parents found out his email address and sent it to me. I contacted Dave and found out that he was only about a mile away from me. We met and began talking. Dave was a committed Christian and was striving to serve God. Because he and his fellow civilian contractors were working 12-14+ hour days, seven days a week, they were unable to attend chapel services. Only a few weeks before we met, Dave had begun gathering with two other men late on a Sunday night for a Bible study. He invited me to the study the next Sunday.

As I entered the dimly lit tent where they were meeting, I found three men weary physically, but who loved and were hungry for more of God. As they opened the Bible up and began to study it, we all began to be filled with strength. After they completed the night's study, I ask them, "Have you considered spending a little time worshipping and singing praises to God before studying the Bible?" Dave looked at me and said, "We'd like to, but none of us know how to lead it." I smiled and said, "It just 'so happens' that I've got some experience doing that." The three men smiled too, and said they'd love to sing at the next Sunday's study time. I also asked them to pray and ask God if He wanted us to do more.

The next Sunday night came and we met again in the tent. This time I brought my laptop. I had a few music CDs recorded on the hard drive for us to sing with. We began singing and the presence of God filled that tent! After singing and then studying the Bible for a little while, I intently looked each of them in the eyes. "Have you considered having a structured worship service right here, late Sunday night?" They said "We'd love to, but none of us knows how." I said, "It just 'so happens' that I have some experience in doing that." We planned on having our first worship service the following Sunday night.

The next Sunday night, six men showed up for our first worship service. It was a powerful time of worship, studying the Word of God and being encouraged in our faith by each other! At the end of the service I told the men that I believed God was starting a work, right in our midst! I told them I believed He had begun a church, right there north of Baghdad, and that He wanted me to pastor it! It was an incredibly humbling feeling. I remember often saying to myself, "This is what the 'big boys' of the faith do. They pioneer churches in difficult situations. God must have a lot of faith in me to give me this chance." I knew that there was no way for me to have brought everything together to allow the church to be birthed and grow. It was nothing short of a move of God!

As the weeks turned to months, God was blessing the new church. Every Sunday night I and my chaplain assistant would put our body armor on and make the drive along the base perimeter (only feet from the fence where the enemy often lurked) to get to where the church was meeting. I would drive so my chaplain assistant could keep his M-16 ready to respond if we can under attack. The numbers of people coming grew almost weekly. We soon lost the tent we were meeting in, and began to pray for a new meeting place. Before the next service, we were given permission to meet in the main conference room in the contractor's headquarters! We soon grew to capacity in that location. Numerous services I had to preach while turning in a circle, because there were so many people surrounding me and standing shoulder to shoulder. We had to move and stack all the furniture in a corner to make more room for people!

It was an incredible bunch of men and women to pastor! People were getting saved and people came hungry for God. There was no cheer leading necessary when I started service. All I had to do was let them loose to praise God and Heaven came down to our congregation!

Each week I gave all I had to minister to those entrusted to my care. I did feel God giving me strength, but I was still pouring out faster than I could take in. I could only do that so long.

One of the greatest group of men & women a pastor could serve!
This was after one of our worship services and fellowship times, which ended about 10:30 at night! These were the ones who stayed through it all and saw God move, including Dave, seated to my right! Shortly after this picture was taken, attendance exploded! We had to remove and then replace all of the tables and chairs each service to fit all the people!

With about two months to go on the deployment, I hit a wall. I felt I could go no further. I was exhausted, physically, emotionally, and even spiritually. I was ministering daily to those traumatized by the horrors of war. Soldiers and Airmen daily came to me to unload their burdens, often describing death and destruction that would haunt them, and me. And mortars and rockets flew over me, too. One night I lay in my bunk watching a DVD episode of M.A.S.H. on my laptop. At the same moment the 4077th came under attack on the episode, we came under attack! (Talk about realistic TV!) I heard the distinctive sound of an incoming missile overhead! I rolled out of the bunk and grabbed my body armor as the missile impacted a hundred yards past my tent. I imagined I felt a lot like Elijah after seeing God work mightily on Mt. Carmel. Not long after that, Elijah cried out to God in desperation and exhaustion. I did the same.

One night, in the chapel sanctuary, I cried out to God, telling Him I couldn't go any further. I was exhausted. I prayed that He would bring me back home to my family. I prayed that He would take this struggle away from me. After twenty or thirty minutes of soul anguish, I finally had poured my whole heart out to God. Then I knew enough to be quiet and listen to what God might say back.

In my heart and mind I began to think about the Apostle Paul's prayer for Christ to remove a 'thorn' in his flesh that was a torment to him. Three times Paul prayed to have it removed, and three times the Lord said basically the same thing; "No!" I felt God say the same thing to me that night in Iraq. But He didn't leave me with that. He also said what He said to Paul, found in 2 Corinthians 12:9. "My grace is sufficient for you, for my power is made perfect in weakness."

At that moment I understood God's Grace in a whole new way. Even though I grew up in the Church, my understanding of God's Grace was always tied to salvation exclusively. It was 'by grace' we were saved. As absolutely true as that was, it does not sum up all of what 'Grace' really is. The passage in 2 Corinthians 12 shows that Paul was clearly already saved when Jesus spoke those words. Paul had already relied on God's saving Grace. Now he needed to rely on God's sustaining and empowering Grace. And that's the Grace I needed to continue serving God and others in Iraq and after.

I would love to say that I only saw smooth sailing after that night, but that would not be true. Something fundamental had changed in me, but I still had to face the realities of my life. However, that night I 'got it.' I

22

understood why Paul said in 2 Corinthians 12:10, "For when I am weak, then I am strong."

I continued to care for my military and civilian flocks and felt God's strength in my weaknesses. I continued to minister to those tragically wounded and dying in the field hospital there, being with several as they breathed their last and entered eternity. God's strength and providence was most pronounced in the young Contractors' Church. As we maxed out the room we were meeting in, we began praying for God to give us a larger facility, knowing that it's a lot harder to get one in a war zone than in Hometown, USA. However, we had seen God do so much already. We knew He would do it somehow.

As the months moved on and my time for coming home drew close, we still did not have a new home. Because we were literally standing shoulder to shoulder weekly in the service, some people decided not to come back. We were in danger of being a victim of our own success. We also did not have anyone to lead the church when I left. At that point, all Army chaplains were prohibited from entering the contractors' camp, so no Army chaplain could pastor the congregation. All three of us Air Force chaplains were leaving and the Air Force commander had indicated that he may make the camp off limits to Air Force personnel too.

12/25/2003

Above: Christmas 2003 with family...Where's John?
As happens every Christmas, members of the military
are away from their loved ones to defend us all
Below: Ready in my bunk for Christmas in Iraq

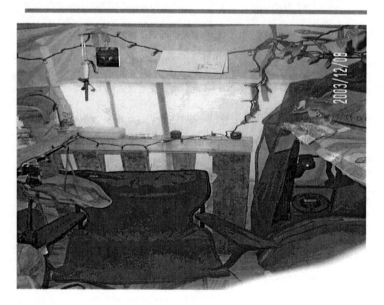

2003/12/08

If we did not get a larger facility and a new pastor, we were facing the end of the church that had been birthed right there. We needed God to provide! And He did.

During the service on the second Sunday before I was to redeploy back home, Jim, one of the new leaders of the church, stood during service to testify. Over the months, we had been hearing about God healing bodies, hearts and marriages during our time there. We had seen God provide for us in so many ways. We just knew God would provide us a place to meet. Jim stood and told us that the contractor had begun construction of a multipurpose building that would seat 250 people and would be completed within the following few weeks. He then said, "We've been given permission to meet in there and have been given priority access for our Sunday night services!" God had provided a new home for His church! Now 'all' we needed was a new pastor.

That week came and went with no new pastor. We came to the last Sunday worship service before I was to leave on Tuesday. There was joy and sadness in all of us. God had already done so much in our midst. We couldn't stand the thought of it dying for lack of a leader. But finding a pastor in the war zone of Iraq was not an easy prospect. There were no "Want Ads" to advertise in. Only God could bring in the person to shepherd His flock there.

As the worship service drew to a close, we prayed again for God to provide a new pastor and then had a time of eating cookies and snacks sent from back home in the States. As I was eating and chatting, Dave came up to me with a man next to him. Dave said, "John, this is Glen. He just arrived here two days ago and has something to tell you."

As I shook Glen's hand, he said, "John, I'm a bi-vocational pastor. When I took the contract to come to Iraq and work, I felt like God had another purpose for me being here. Until now, I didn't know what it was. But now I believe I do. I believe God wants me to pastor this service when you leave." *Almost* Unbelievable!!! At the end of the last service before I left the country, God brought an ordained minister to pastor the Church that He had begun right there north of Baghdad, Iraq! I left Iraq both knowing God in a new and powerful way and being exhausted at the same time. My cup overflowed, from both good and bad. I was fracturing and I did not realize it.

I arrived back home in Arizona to a bit of a surprise. When the Air Force canceled my orders to go remote to Thule, Greenland, they had not canceled the orders of my replacement at Davis-Monthan. Within a month of my deploying to Iraq, my replacement arrived at the base. He was given all my duties and began ministering to his new flock. When I arrived back on base, I had no worship service to pastor and no units to minister in. I had no purpose to drive me.

I had been dealing with life and death almost daily for months. Coming home, I had nothing to deal with. Many people would say that should have been a relief for me. But, anyone who has been to war knows, coming home is difficult.

Within a few weeks, I received orders to move to Keesler Air Force Base in Biloxi, Mississippi.

Maybe things would be better there…

2003/10/08

The picture that sustained me through my deployment. It hung on my bunk, in my office, and I carried a copy with me everywhere I went

4

THE LORD GIVES:
THE LORD TAKES

About nine months after arriving at Keesler and one year after returning home from Iraq, my third child, and first son was born! I dearly loved my daughters and I was so excited to have my son! When he was two and a half months old, he began running a high fever. I took him to the Emergency Room. After examining him and taking a spinal tap, they concluded he had Spinal Meningitis and admitted him to Pediatric Intensive Care. Over the next week, little Timothy endured countless tests and the numerous pricks and IV needles stuck in him, as he struggled for life. The doctors were trying to save his life. As I held my little boy in my arms, with wires and tubes all over his tiny body, my heart ached and I so much wanted to trade places with him. "Why, God?" I cried out! But no answer came.

The Sunday he was in the hospital was Mothers' Day. With not a word of complaint, Terri, the wonderful mother she was and is, stayed with Timothy around the clock. As I watched her holding our baby, I thanked God for such a wonderful wife and mother to our kids. I wanted to be a good dad to them. Since it was Sunday, I took my daughters to church. I didn't have responsibilities at the chapel that Sunday, so I took them to our church off-base. We came in and sat on the back row. Part of me wanted to be with Timothy, part of me wanted to be anywhere but there, and part of me wanted to be nowhere but there. My son was hanging between life and death. Would he live? Would God save my boy's life?

As I sat there on the back row, I began to cry. My heart was so heavy. I wanted to pray. I wanted to convince God to save my son. But I didn't know what to pray. What do you pray to get the attention of the Creator of the whole universe? As I sat weeping, two of the men of the church came over, lay their hands on me and began to pray for me. As they began to pray, I felt a power come on me.[1] I felt empowered to pray. Although part of me wanted to pray some powerful and impressive prayer to convince God to save my son, another part of me just wanted to bow in the presence of God. I was faced with a decision. Could I convince God to save my son or would I throw myself at the

---

[1] I've come to believe that it was a gift of Grace from God.

mercy of God and trust Him? Within seconds, I had made my decision. I looked up to Heaven and prayed, "I trust you God!" Over and over again I prayed, "I trust you God!" Each time I prayed it, more peace came on me. God did not tell me if my son would live or die. But He told me that I could trust Him. I did, and I learned more about God's Grace. Early the next morning, the doctors told us that Timothy was improving. Within three days, we brought him home! God had saved my son's life!

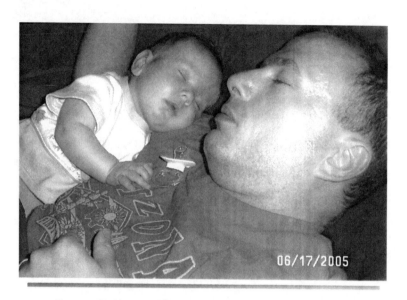

Above: Exhausted by life and the brush with Tim's death, Dad and Tim catch a few winks

Left: Just over a month after Timothy got out of the hospital, we celebrated our tenth wedding anniversary with a renewal of our vows

5

CAUGHT BY HURRICANE KATRINA

I was overjoyed to have my son back home! But staring at death in the face again exposed something deep within me that tied me back to Iraq. I began experiencing what I could only describe as 'dark areas' of my life. I reacted to things in ways that were very uncharacteristic of me. I had very little patience and was easily startled. I would wake up every morning with the sheets soaked with sweat from my nightmares the night before. After struggling with those feelings for months, while sitting in my supervisor's office, I came to realize that I needed help. As I described what I was feeling, my boss said "John, that sounds a lot like Post Traumatic Stress Disorder. Maybe you should ask for help from those best able to help you with that." That caring response ultimately drove me to seek help and be diagnosed in late May 2005 with Post-Traumatic Stress Disorder (PTSD) from Iraq.

Over the next weeks I began to get help in dealing with PTSD. However, when the monster Hurricane Katrina roared ashore that Monday, August 29th, 2005, she grabbed my gaze and transfixed it for months after. I could focus on nothing else. She would force me down a road I had never traveled before and challenge me in ways I had never known. What follows is the story of those days and weeks that forever changed me and my family. Hurricane Katrina brought devastation on an unprecedented scale. My family and I sheltered on base for the storm and had to remain there for eight days, until cleared to evacuate my family to safety and return for reconstruction. From dealing with a suicidal person in the shelter during the storm to kicking open doors in destroyed houses and trying to comfort those who had lost everything and from holding my dying baby boy in my arms to loading a shotgun to protect my family, new wounds were piled on to the still open old ones. With the base hospital and its Mental Health Clinic out of commission, my unseen war wounds would have to wait.

THE FATEFUL DECISIONS

Nearly one year before Katrina, my family had evacuated from Hurricane Ivan and spent twenty hours on the road, while I spent one night in the base shelter. (Each shelter had one chaplain assigned, to care for the 800+ shelterees.) My pregnant wife, two daughters, two cats and a dog all took to the road to 'safety' with a pregnant friend, her son and dog and hundreds of thousands of others. Because Ivan turned east and did not hit us, I left the shelter and went home before my wife and children had made it safely to family in Texas.

When Hurricane Dennis came calling the month before Katrina, we decided to keep the family together and sheltered on base. We were only in the shelter six hours before being released. Those experiences would prove to be fateful, as it influenced our decision with Katrina.

K-2[†]

The day was to be different than other Saturdays. We were going to participate in the American Heart Association's "Walk for Life" in Gulfport, Mississippi. One of our chaplain's sons was born with a heart defect and the whole staff was going out to show our support for him and all the work of the AHA.

We parked right off of Highway 90/Beach Boulevard in Gulfport, right next to First Baptist Church of Gulfport. The beach was only a couple hundred yards away.

As we were walking with hundreds of other people, we began to hear about a hurricane that was nearing Florida and might affect us in Mississippi. Immediately our concern went up a level.

As we finished the walk and began to drive home down Highway 90, we decided to stop at the Wendy's by the mall and get some lunch. As we sat in the van to eat, I received a call from the chapel superintendent. He told me of the Crisis Action Team (CAT) meeting that would be held

---

[†] *Time designations in military operations or major events are often designated in relation to the start of the operation or event (e.g. Katrina = K). Events happening the day before would be designated K-1.*

in a few hours to discuss Hurricane Katrina and the base's possible evacuation. I was then put on telephone standby, needing to be ready to respond when needed.

We went home and began preparations. Considering our experiences with Hurricanes Ivan and Dennis, if the evacuation order was given, we decided to have the whole family shelter on base. The order was given within a few hours.

We were to report to the shelter in Jones Hall by 1630 on Sunday evening and bring supplies for three days. Surely that would be more than enough?!

K - 1

As Sunday came, so did news that Katrina was turning into a behemoth, with incredible power, and an eye for Mississippi. Our concern went up a few more levels.

After canceling worship services on base and having a morning staff meeting of all the chaplains and chaplain assistants who would be sheltering, we each went to our homes to finish preparations and report to the shelters. I dropped by the Base Exchange store to pick up a few last minute items. As I was heading to check out, I saw a display of small battery operated camping fans. I dropped one in the cart, thinking "It wouldn't hurt to have one of these if the power goes out." I didn't realize how important it would become.

We loaded the van with the provisions and prepared to leave for the unknown. With no good option for our pets, we decided to leave them at home. I locked our dog in the bathroom and put her bed, food and water in the bath tub. If the house flooded, at least she would have a dry place, I thought. I was less concerned about the cat. She could climb up anywhere to get away from the rising water. Or could she?

We arrived at the shelter and began setting up our 'home' in a classroom. The desks had been stacked against the wall and we set up beds in the middle. This would be my family's home for the next four days and mine for the next five.

I set out to establish links with the shelter management team. Thankfully, I had been their chaplain for a year and had already sheltered with them twice.

As hundreds of people entered our 'ark', people were in good spirits.

We all settled in for the first night in Noah's Ark Hotel.

K – DAY

KATRINA HITS WITH A VENGEANCE!

The next morning we were awakened in the morning by the howling of the wind through the cracks in the doors. Katrina was there.

The winds howled all day. We lost power sometime that morning. Emergency generator power was supplied to strategic rooms, to ensure power to vital communication and lights. I was able to see outside and watched as the trees were bent back and forth. However, other than some small debris blowing around, there appeared to be little damage out those few windows. "Maybe this would not be so bad, after all," I thought.

I occupied myself throughout the day taking care of my people, the inhabitants of our 'Jones Hilton,' as we called it. Dozens of us crowded in a small room to watch the only working TV. On it we watched as pictures of the area, our neighborhoods and shopping areas, were flashed. We were sheltered inside. What was happening out there? Anxieties ran high throughout the shelter. I was called to rooms throughout the shelter to talk with extremely anxious people. One of those rooms led me to deal with a suicidal person.

As I counseled with him and worked through his concerns, I was able to bring him back to the side of life. The weight on my shoulders was increasing.

My concerns went even higher.

Being locked inside the building and as the day drew to a close, there was nothing to do but try to get some sleep. Something told us we would need it tomorrow.

K + 1

As Tuesday morning dawned, I was called to a shelter management team meeting. The shelter commander (a man I had respected before the experience, but who took that respect to a whole new high during and after) told us that early damage reports had come back in and things did not look good. He said the base and surrounding areas had seen incredible damage. He told us that we would probably be in the shelter for an additional four days. My concerns rose again.

With more than 40 children sheltering in Jones, I knew something needed to be done to keep them occupied and out of trouble. After securing permission from the commander, I took over his conference room and turned it into a kids' entertainment hub. I sent word out throughout the shelter, requesting DVDs of children's movies and asking if there were any game systems that could be used by the kids. A PS2 was offered and dozens of movies were brought. Thus began Jones' Fun Park. After working out a schedule of volunteers to run it, I moved on to other ministry opportunities. There were many.

Since most people only brought supplies for three days, we would quickly run out of vital supplies of baby formula and diapers for the youngest among us. Our Contracting officers were dispatched to the destroyed Commissary to 'requisition' any supplies that were usable. They came back with sealed diapers and formula that had been on top shelves. They would have to sustain us until relief supplies could be brought in.

COMM CHAOS

Communication about the world outside the shelter was infrequent and vague. Were our houses standing? Did we have places to go home to? Reports and rumors began coming in.

Regular telephone lines were all down. Only Defense Switched Network (DSN) phones worked, and they worked only sporadically. With those I was only able to call other military bases. From those bases, I was able to use a calling card to call my family in Texas, to let them know we were OK.

Much of base housing had been flooded by the storm surge. One house had exploded and burned down during the storm. Debris littered all streets. It was not yet safe for us to leave the shelter.

Meanwhile, the temperature in the shelters was sweltering. It was so hot and humid that the wax was melting off the tile floors. The walls were all sweating. It was very dangerous to walk around the shelter. People were falling everywhere, unable to get traction on the extremely slippery floors.

We were told that single Non Prior Service students were going to be airlifted away from the base within hours. They were told to pack what they could carry in a bag and leave everything else behind. Rather than have all those supplies and belongings thrown away, I turned my room into a collection point for donations. All that came in would be given to those who had lost everything. Everything from food and drinks to computers and stereo equipment were brought in. The generosity of so many was evident to all who came to my room.

As I heard the reports, I could not help but wonder about my home. Was it still there? Was it flooded? I lived a little more than fifty yards from the Back Bay. I could not help but wonder about my pets. Were they alive or dead?

K + 2

Wednesday came and we were told one person from each family would be permitted to go inspect their home and then report back to the shelter. We would have one hour to view the homes and return to the shelter. We were to team up with a Wingman, since it was still uncertain as to the safety of the houses. We were to never be alone. I teamed with the shelter doctor, Dr. Michael Kinney, a fellow captain and friend.

As we boarded the bus to be taken to base housing, anxieties were escalating. Tensions were raw. What would we find? How would we tell our families what we saw?

As we began driving around the base, we could see the incredible destruction. Trees were down everywhere. Fences and buildings were torn apart. Debris lined the streets. Only a single lane had been cleared for the buses to get through.

As we approached base housing, everyone caught sight of the first house. It was missing the bottom half of three walls. Actually, they were not missing. They were strewn all around the yard. Brick walls were shattered.

Michael pointed to the house we were looking at and spoke barely above a whisper, "That's my house."

As we continued and I looked out the window, I saw houses with walls missing. I saw cars thrown across yards with debris everywhere. The route the bus had to take (the route blazed by the fire trucks) took us by my house first. As we got off the bus, I spotted my house. It appeared to be OK, at least from the outside. We awkwardly made our way through the thick black mud that had been left behind by Katrina. Tree limbs and other debris were in front of my front door. I noticed the debris line was right up to the door. What would I find behind that door? Were the cat and dog dead? Was there anything left?

GUILTY THANKS

I removed the debris, put my key in the door and turned the knob. I opened the door to hear the sound of the dog yipping and saw the cat trotting to meet me. All else was as it was when we left it on Sunday! The flood had literally stopped at my doorstep! There was no damage inside!

As we left my house and headed for Michael's, I felt joy and sadness, relief and guilt. My house had been saved! Michael's was not. My pets and everything in my house were OK. Why was my house saved and not Michael's? I had no answers. I felt thankful, but I also felt guilty for not having lost everything.

NOT SO 'LUCKY'

The heat was almost unbearable. The smell was sickening. Dead fish and other sea creatures littered the streets. But we had to continue on. We knew Captain Kinney's house had not fared well, but now we would go inside.

We walked up the driveway and saw the water line four or five feet up the wall. We tried to open the kitchen door, but it would not budge. We peered inside to see that the refrigerator had been washed in front of the door. We could see that the sofa had been washed in front of the front door. We would have to force our way in.

With both of us pushing with all of our strength, we were able to push the refrigerator enough to allow us to squeeze inside. The appliances had been tossed around the house as if they were children's toys. A sorrow, unlike any I had ever felt, bowed my heart low as I stood next to my friend and walked with him through his destroyed house.

After seeing what valuables could be salvaged and taking many pictures with my digital camera to show his wife, Michael and I began to walk back to wait for the bus.

As we walked, we came across a group that had just gotten off a bus a few minutes before. They had not yet gone into their homes. When they saw that I was a Chaplain, many asked if I would go with them into their homes. It was in that moment that I truly was able to be a "visible reminder of the Holy". People who had never met me, nor attended church, wanted God's representative with them as they surveyed the results that this fallen world produces.

I entered house after house, kicking doors in to get into this one, climbing through holes in walls in that one. Several of the people I went in with were wives whose husbands were deployed. They would try to deal with the destruction without the help of a spouse nearby. I provided a shoulder to cry on as they saw their prized china shattered all across the house from where it should have been. My shirt was further drenched with tears as they picked up priceless family photos that had been awash in grimy sea water. I knew enough to know that no words were right at moments like these. Silent tears shed in understanding were the salve of the soul now.

With each house the pain I felt intensified. I did not want to enter any more devastated houses. I had to shut off my own emotions in order to be able to help others. I wanted to run away. But I could not leave my people to suffer alone.

I was called by God to be in the world of these people to bring His love and comfort at that time. When God wanted us to really know of His love, He came into our world and suffered with us. That day, in the heat and stench, was the closest I have ever come to understanding what the Incarnation of God was really like. God could have stayed out of the mud and pain, but He chose to clothe Himself in flesh and blood like us and stand with us in the midst of it all, in order to show His love. I did not choose to be there at that time. I believe God put me there to demonstrate God's love.

"The King will reply, 'Truly I tell you, whatever you did for one of the least of these brothers and sisters of mine, you did for me." Matthew 25:40

INCARNATION COSTS

I returned to the shelter emotionally and physically drained. I walked into the room where my family was and saw my wife brace herself for news. She later told me that she had prepared herself to hear that we had lost everything. When I told her the good news, she cried. Days of anxiety spilled out. As we both cried, we thanked God for His blessings on us. We now knew about the past. But our future was still uncertain.

I spent the remainder of the day ministering to those returning from viewing their homes. Some had pictures of the destruction to show. Others had mementos of what used to be. All had stories to tell. I looked at the pictures, asked about the meaning of the mementos, but mostly just listened to the stories. They were windows into the souls of my hurting people. I had to look in. People would finish telling me their story and say "Thanks for listening Chaplain. I just needed to tell someone." We were in it together. We were caught by Katrina.

Our neighbor's house after Katrina washed everything away from inside

K + 3

The next morning, Thursday, we arose and began another 'normal' day in chaos. About mid-morning, we were told that those of us who had habitable homes were going to be released from the shelter and could return to our homes. We were told that we would be 'on our own' for supplies and protection. The shelters were being converted into dorms for the thousands of relief workers who were pouring into the area.

[While we waited, I called my mother and asked if she could get food, clothes and other relief supplies together. As I expected, she eagerly agreed and quickly either bought or collected from others hundreds of dollars of supplies. Although I did not know what supplies were available locally, I knew my family would all they could to provide all we needed. My dad and brother even volunteered to drive it all over to us. They were a very great blessing to us during such a stressful time. I knew I could call on them, and they answered the call.]

After lunch we packed up our belongings and headed for our home. There was no power in the house, but then again, we did not have power at the shelter. At least at home we would have all the toys and beds of our own.

The heat was incredible. Each one of my kids were suffering the effects of severe heat and humidity. We were having them drink lots of water, but nothing would cool them down. Six month old Timothy was red all over from the heat. My wife was using the little camping fan I had bought at the Base Exchange to try to cool him down. It was scary to think about him getting worse. He was already listless. If he got worse, there was nowhere to take him. The base hospital had been flooded. There was nowhere to go for help. We had to take care of him. We kept putting water on him and kept the heat at bay. Would he be OK? Only God knew.

Our neighbors on the other side of our duplex, the Loftons, were good friends of ours. Del, the military member, was TDY at the time, so his wife sheltered at his job with their two sons. They were also released to go to their house on Thursday. As we met up Thursday afternoon, we all began to tell stories of our experiences over the last several days. But at least we were home now. Things would be better. Or so we thought…

I returned to duty at the shelter later in the afternoon and continued organizing relief efforts both from within the shelter, as well as from within the Fishbowl Student Ministry Center chapel facility. About a half hour before sunset I was speaking with shelter management team members when I was grabbed by my boss. He told me that I was not released to my home, but was to stay in the shelter that night. With all communication lines out, I had to drive to my house to tell my wife, and I had to be back to the shelter by sunset.

I raced to my house and grabbed my supplies for the night. I did not want to leave my family, but there was no time to get all the supplies for all the kids loaded back up and back to the shelter in just a few minutes. So Terri and I decided that she and the kids would stay at the house and I would go back to the shelter. Although, in hindsight, I see there were other choices, at the time, I only saw the only choices as staying with my family and disobeying a lawful order or leaving my family to fend for themselves and me to return to the shelter. I chose 'duty' over protecting my family. That is a decision that haunted me for years. It was also the source of major trauma and a sense of betrayal that Terri felt toward me.

The security situation on base was tenuous at that point. Parts of the perimeter fence were down and angry people could be heard shouting from outside the fence that was up near base housing. Apparently, there was a rumor

56

downtown that Keesler had fared well during the storm and just was not helping the local community. That led to flared tempers and tensions. Not knowing what would happen throughout the night, knowing my wife could not communicate with me until I returned at daylight, and knowing I was responsible for my family, I pulled my wife aside, took out the twelve gauge shotgun and gave her a crash course on using it. "If anyone tries to break in or hurt you all, shoot to kill," I heard myself tell her. Even as I was saying the words, I could not help but think, "This is the United States, in Mississippi. This is not Bagdad! I should not have to do this here!" With those thoughts on my mind and with a word of prayer with family, I left them and headed back for a sleepless night in the shelter.

K + 4

I arose at first light the next morning, Friday, and hurried back to the house. Terri had slept very little throughout the night. With no wind at all, every noise had roused her. She had kept the little fan blowing on the baby throughout the night, until the batteries ran down.

There had been two men in civilian clothes that had been walking down the street at about two in the morning. There had been people screaming just outside the fence line. There was uncertainty all around, but God had protected my family. What I had failed to do, God had done.

I had to report back for work later that morning. Early in the afternoon my boss came by again and told me there had been a mistake. No one should be staying in base housing. They had not been inspected for safety. He told me I had to get my family out right away.

I rushed home, packed them up as quickly as possible and headed back to the shelter area. Having been taken out of the shelter and assigned to the Fishbowl, which had become the hub of relief efforts for the base, I secured permission to move my family into the Fishbowl. We took over the Spouses' Lounge and made it into our new 'home.'

There was still no air conditioning, but a large generator had been brought in and supplied all other power to the building. At least we would have electric fans that night.

There was word that a team of chaplains and chaplain assistants would be deploying in soon, but no word yet when they would arrive. I was told that when they arrived, and it was safe to leave the base, I could evacuate my family and return for duty.

At a 'town hall' meeting called by the wing commander, we were told that dependents were to be evacuated and set up in a 'safe haven' for 'the long haul'. No one knew how long that was, but we were told to prepare for at least six months. There was also talk going around that Keesler would now be a deployed location, or even a remote assignment. Once our families left, it may be a long time before we could see them.

The thought that I could be on a remote assignment, right in Mississippi boggled my mind and my anxiety rose even higher into the red zone.

HEARTACHE AND TOUGH CHOICES

As I sat and talked with scores upon scores of people coming and going through the Fishbowl that day and the next couple days, I could not help but wonder what the future would hold. I heard stories of having to leave pets behind in homes while the family was flown away. I heard stories of evacuations happening within two hours of notification. They were sitting and waiting to see what was going to happen, and then two hours later they were on a plane, not knowing when or even if they were coming back.

During those days, we had numerous high profile visitors to the Fishbowl. The Secretary of Defense came with the Chairman of the Joint Chiefs. Senators and Congressmen came. Even President Bush came. It was nice to meet them and shake their hands, but I wanted to get away and get my family to safety.

I was torn between my duties to protect and care for my family and my duties to Keesler. I needed to get my family to safety, so that I could pass off that responsibility to others who could help. On Saturday, I was told that the incoming Angel One Team (as we dubbed them) would arrive Sunday morning. I was told I would have to stay another day and then I would be allowed to leave to evacuate my family Monday morning, eight days after we first sheltered. I remember being very angry with the wing chaplain, because there was no good reason not to let me take my family out on Sunday. If I did not already have a great respect for the man, that decision would have severed the friendship I was so glad to have. However, after settling down, I thought, "We've been here seven days, what's one more." I was given two weeks to get my family set up in a home and then I had to return for duty.

The iconic Biloxi Lighthouse (above) and the Shark Head souvenir shop (below) after Katrina, as seen from the Marine helicopter I flew missions with.

Buildings are all gone!

TRIAL ON THE ROAD

Monday, Labor Day, came and we anxiously and excitedly headed out for the Deer Park, Texas area, where my family lives. We planned to lease a house, rent furniture and enroll my daughter, Danielle, in her second school in a month, her first month of kindergarten.

We were well into Louisiana when the van began to jerk and sputter. The transmission light came on and I knew we were in trouble. It was too far to turn back, but we were not even close to our destination. We pulled off at the next exit and tried to find a service station. Since it was Labor Day, we were having difficulty finding one open. I stopped at a Wal-Mart Super Center and explained what had happened. They did not know who to suggest, but a customer who was standing nearby thought he did. He recommended an Auto Zone about a block away. After jerking and sputtering over there, we were told that they could do nothing. However, they recommended a garage about two miles away, and thought they were open.

We drove down the road and found the shop open. We pulled in and I went in to seek help. The owner came out with a vehicle code reader and read the codes on the van.

63

He told us that an important sensor on the transmission was going out and would have to be replaced. When I explained our situation to him, he said he could reset the codes and they might stay off long enough for us to get to Texas. Staying in that town until the transmission was fixed was not a viable option for us. I asked him to go ahead and reset the codes. With codes reset and the light gone, we headed back down the highway toward our 'safe haven.'

We had gone another couple hours when the transmission light came back on and the jerking and sputtering started up. This time the air conditioner went out. We had no air conditioning on a sweltering September day. The van was full with all the household goods we could carry, all of the pets, three worn out children and two exhausted adults and we were still a couple hours away from our destination! We had to press on! We were praying and called ahead and had all our families praying. After a very long and very stressful trip, we pulled into my parent's house late that night. We had arrived at a safe haven. God had taken care of us!

We unloaded the van into my parents' house and went to bed. I do not remember getting into the bed, but I woke up in one the next day. We were exhausted!

SHOP TALK

The next morning I found a Honda dealer to take the van into. I drove it in and, after diagnosing it for a day, was told that I would need a new transmission. Furthermore, as they were checking the van over, they found out the air conditioner compressor would also have to be replaced. We had cracked motor mounts from the trip, as well as several other problems. All in all, it would be about $6000 worth of repairs! Just add that to what had already happened! We were numb.

It took just over a week for the repairs to be completed. We were given a loaner car, so it was only an inconvenience, rather than a major problem. As we braced for the total, we were rejoicing that it ended up that the transmission was under recall from Honda, so they would be picking up the cost of rebuilding of the transmission! The rest of the repairs were also covered by an extended warranty that we had on the van. We ended up owing just about nothing when we picked up the van! God had taken care of it, again!

As my time in Texas was drawing to a close, we finally found a nice house, only a couple minutes from my parents. We signed the lease, rented or bought some furniture and moved in. With that anxiety pouring into me, I had to head back to Keesler and the ongoing relief efforts.

A picture I took of the mall in Gulfport, Mississippi while I was on a mission with the Marines ... Nothing but the foundation was left of the restaurant we ate at two days before Katrina.

STARED DOWN BY
HURRICANE RITA

On 20 September, I flew on a mission with the Marines down the Mississippi and Louisiana coasts and into New Orleans. While on that mission I heard about the preparations there for a possible hit by Hurricane Rita, a new monster hurricane in the Gulf and heading for Texas. I got in contact with Terri in Texas and found out that the principal of the school my daughter had been going to had sent a note home on Tuesday, saying that school was canceled the rest of the week, due to Hurricane Rita. At that time, Hurricane Rita was intensifying and turned into a huge category 5 storm. It looked like it would directly hit Galveston, Texas, which would put Terri and the kids in the top right quadrant, the deadliest. We knew it was only a matter of time before an evacuation would be ordered for Deer Park, as it is right on the Houston Ship Channel and would most likely flood in a category 4 or 5 storm surge. With the lessons of Katrina fresh on our minds, Terri and I decided for her to pack up what she could and evacuate, yet again. Keesler was still off limits for families, so they couldn't come home to stay. We decided that they would evacuate to Pensacola, Florida, where we had friends. Terri loaded everything up and headed to Florida on 21 September, about twelve hours before evacuations began in Houston.

The evacuations in Houston were the largest ever in the United States. Probably millions of people were trying to get out of the Houston area and away from Rita's fury. Each area of town was given its own evacuation corridors and time schedule. The freeways were in gridlock. It took many people twelve to fourteen hours to get what should have taken less than an hour. Fear was beginning to grip the city. I was informed of it all by all my family in Houston. My sister and brother in law and their family were trying to evacuate, only to end up turning around, due to the gridlock and dwindling gas supplies. When it was time for my parents to evacuate, their corridor was shut down when a bus of elderly people caught fire while sitting on the freeway. All on board were killed. As Rita neared landfall, my family all decided to ride out the storm at their homes. There was no other choice.

Thankfully, Rita turned east, missing Houston with the worst of the damage. My family lost power for several hours during the night and had a little bit of damage. Other than that, everyone was fine.

I felt Rita's fury, even back in Biloxi. Rita tore off many of the tarps that were put on roofs after Katrina. My office at the chapel had received relatively little damage during Katrina. However, during Rita, areas of the roof were torn off and water drenched my office.

Two days after Rita roared through Texas and Louisiana, after hearing that our rental house in Deer Park had only lost the fence, Terri and the kids returned to the 'Safe Haven' in Texas.

Evacuee Danielle in her second school in the first three months of kindergarten

SURGERY IMMINENT?

The next week, I got a call from my wife, telling me that she had another pain attack more intense than the ones she had been dealing with for months.

She had already had numerous tests at Keesler and was scheduled to have the results read on the day Katrina hit. She had gone into a doctor in Houston on a Thursday and was told she needed a surgery as soon as possible. They would wait until the next Tuesday, so I could arrive, but no longer. I hurriedly got emergency leave and raced over to be with her. The surgery went well, but the doctor said she had not corrected the problem. Only time would tell if the pain would come back. After a few days for her recovery, I had to go back to Keesler.

PAINFUL HOME COMING

This whole time, there was no word as to when, or even if, the military dependents would be recalled to Keesler. It was now mid-October and everything was back to normal at my Keesler house. The power was back on and all debris was removed. We saw no reason to keep our family separated. When word went out that families were 'permitted' to return, we set the date for 1 November as the return date. We gave notice to the landlord and rental store and set our minds and hearts on reunion in a matter of weeks.

As time drew down to a few days, Terri began to experience the excruciating pain once again. We knew she would need surgery. However, with only a couple days left in the rental house, there would be nowhere to recover, since she would not be able to travel after the surgery. Terri and I decided it would be best for us to make it back to Mississippi and have the surgery there, where she could recover at home. And that is what we did.

On 1 November, Terri and the kids returned to Mississippi. The next day Terri got in to see an OB/GYN in Biloxi. (Every OB/GYN on base had been moved away due to the damage to the base hospital.) After reviewing the results from the earlier tests, as well as the results from the surgery in Texas, he decided that they should immediately remove Terri's right ovary and fallopian tube. With what we saw as such a radical choice, we decided to seek a second opinion. The next day we were able to get an appointment with a doctor in Gulfport. After viewing the results and talking with Terri, he suggested the same course of action. That was the only way to keep the pain from coming back. Although he assured us that it would have no effect on our ability to have the fourth child we wanted, we were concerned. God had seen us through so much already. We had to trust Him to take care of us then.

Surgery was scheduled for the next day. After several hours, the surgery was over. The doctor considered it a success. "Would it be enough to keep the pain away? Would we still be able to have another child?" we anxiously wondered.

WHY GOD?

To the day we left Biloxi, we all still struggled with life at post-Katrina Keesler.

Most restaurants we ate at and most play areas the kids played at were taken by Katrina. Most of our and our kids friends were taken by Katrina related moves following the storm. First Baptist Gulfport (where we had parked for the Heart Walk the Saturday before the storm) had been destroyed. Only the balcony and roof and steel support beams remained. The Wendy's, where we had stopped for lunch on that Saturday before the storm, was destroyed. Only the parking lot and slab remained. Everywhere we went, we were reminded of the destruction. Mounds of debris lined every street we traveled down.

The needs of the base personnel and families, as well as the off-base community were incredibly wide. Just before Katrina I was put in charge of the base's marriage and family ministries and selected to lead the base's Integrated Delivery System (IDS) group, charged with uniting the 'people helping' agencies on base to care for the needs of military personnel and dependents. Those needs taxed every resource we had. The challenges were many, but I had the opportunity to make a positive difference everywhere I turned. Almost every day I had couples at the brink of divorce come into my office. "Why?!" was a question I heard daily, usually through sobs of tears and anguish. "Why did God let this happen?" many would ask me. I often found myself asking the same question in my prayers. I had been trained in seminary and my counseling classes to deal with those questions. However, the level of destruction was just beyond my ability to comprehend. My faith told me that God was saddened by the destruction and, especially, by the loss of life. But I did not have any satisfactory answers. I was in the middle of it too.

6

THE SPIRAL DOWNWARD

For nearly ten months following Katrina, I gave and gave to the seemingly insatiable needs of so many on the base and in the communities around the base. I had placed my wounds from Iraq high on a mental shelf, out of reach for the time. I felt that if I started to deal with them, I would be overwhelmed and unable to help other people with their issues. There was also no longer anyone at Keesler equipped to help me in my struggle. Then I received word of my orders to MacDill Air Force Base in Tampa, Florida.

As I hung up the phone from my boss giving me the news of my orders to move, I could not speak. How could God send me from Biloxi just down the coast to Tampa, which had been threatened by numerous hurricanes just the season before???!!! My cup was cracking.

We arrived, bought our first house and moved in to start this new chapter in our life, hoping to leave Katrina behind. But that would not happen.

After being in Tampa for only a couple of months and no longer being around the devastation and demands of

Post-Katrina Keesler, the feelings that had haunted me from Iraq came back. But this time they were not alone. This time they had much company from Hurricane Katrina.

Though war was raging within me, there was still time to take my girls on Daddy Daughter Date Night

However, I knew I needed help in dealing with them. I had received such compassionate help at Keesler for the short time from when I sought help and when Katrina took away the help. I expected and hoped to get the same help again. With that hope, I set an appointment with a counselor at the base Life Skills Support Center.

I sat down with the counselor and began to pour out what I was dealing with. After a lengthy talk, she diagnosed me with PTSD from Iraq and also from Hurricane Katrina. I was oddly relieved to hear it. But I knew that my journey toward healing had begun.

Because I felt that my abilities were greatly diminished by my struggles, I decided I should tell my supervisor, Chaplain Ortiz‡, and ask for his understanding and help, too. I went to Chaplain Ortiz's office and asked to speak with him. Over the next half hour, I told him of my experiences and that I was getting counseling help for them. I asked for his help, too. He awkwardly thanked me for telling him and I left his office. As I left, I felt that I would regret telling him of my struggles. It felt so odd that, remembering the words of an earlier supervisor to "document everything," I sat down and wrote a Memorandum For Record explaining my concerns, filed it away in my drawers, and hoped to never to see again. Unfortunately, it did not take long for my fears to be realized.

Within the next few weeks, Chaplain Ortiz's attitude towards me changed. He began finding fault in much of what I was doing. Over the following months, he developed a clear bias against me. One morning I went into his office

---

‡ Not his real name. I have done it, not to protect him, but because he is not alone in his way of thinking. Using a pseudonym is intended to represent each person of the minority in the military who project their own personal issues onto others and reinforce the destructive stigma against getting mental health help.

and, as respectfully as possible, asked why he was treating me the way he was. He looked at me and said, "Good chaplains give help. They don't need help. You, obviously, are not a good chaplain." I was flabbergasted! It wasn't because of any poor performance on my part. His bias against me was simply because I needed mental help. Because of the struggles of PTSD, I was already feeling like a failure. His comments and almost daily actions against me continued to hammer at my foundation. He believed I was not a good chaplain, and interpreted seemingly everything I did to prove that assumption.[§] Not only did I have to fight against PTSD, I also had to fight against one who should have helped me. My cup was overflowing and I was breaking further.

Because I felt I was not functioning up to my potential, I also decided to reveal my struggle with PTSD to our small staff during a staff meeting shortly after I revealed the same to Chaplain Ortiz. I simply stated that I had been diagnosed with PTSD and was getting help for it. I asked for grace in dealing with me and, while still holding me accountable for my actions, consider what may lie

---

[§] I later came to learn this was known as 'confirmation bias.' That is when a person starts with a bias and then interprets everything to confirm that the bias was true. I had to learn that this was Chaplain Ortiz's problem, not mine.

underneath any curt words or perceived distance in me. My revelation was met with compassionate looks and words from almost all of the staff present…Almost, but not all.

Over the following months, my Wing Chaplain, Chaplain Stevenson**, put me in charge of several different programs of the chapel. However, three times, while talking in the office with a Chaplain Assistant, I found out that I had been removed from leadership of those same programs by the Wing Chaplain. Unfortunately, Chaplain Stevenson did not tell me, either directly or through my supervisor. The Chaplain Assistants knew about it before I did. After the third time, I asked to speak with Chaplain Stevenson. When I sat down in his office, I told him about the three programs and asked him what I had done to make him lose confidence in me and my abilities. He simply said "Because you revealed to the staff your struggles with PTSD." It was not because of any poor job performance. It was simply because I was struggling with PTSD and also that he didn't think I should have revealed that about myself to the staff. I didn't know how to respond to that. But I did know that I did not have his support to deal with Chaplain Ortiz's ongoing negative treatment of me.

** Not his real name, done for the same reason stated for "Chaplain Ortiz" above.

I slowly walked down the hallways from his office to mine, trying to make sense of what he just told me. But it did not make sense. I believe it would have been easier for me to deal with both of these chaplains' treatment if it were based on failures in my performance, rather than in a perceived fundamental weakness in who I was mentally. I had enough integrity to strive to correct any failures to meet objective standards.

I remember the first base air show I was at MacDill. As a member of the Disaster Control Group for the show, I had to be at the rally point at 7:30 AM the day of the show. I lived off base and had a normal drive of 35-40 minutes to get to base. Expecting heavy traffic that morning, I left an hour and a half before I had to be to the rally point. However, that was not enough time. With traffic heavy and at a snail's pace coming onto the base, I realized that I would not be able to arrive on time. I called Chaplain Ortiz at 7 AM to tell him. Since he was already on base, he told me that he would go to the rally point in my place and that I should come as soon as I could. I finally arrived at the rally point at 8 AM.

I felt guilty. I was clearly not where I was supposed to be when I was supposed to be there. I had tried to be responsible by leaving early, but could not have known the level of traffic that would hinder me from arriving on time. Not wanting to repeat my failure the next morning, I left home two hours early and arrived at the rally point one hour *before* I was supposed to be there. I had made a mistake, but had learned from it and did not make it again. But Chaplain Ortiz did not see it like that. To him, it was another illustration of my mental weakness.

What I could not correct was the perception from my superiors that I had a fundamental mental weakness. For them, I was not guilty of <u>doing</u> wrong. I was guilty of <u>being</u> wrong. I often felt their shame. And shame drove me downward…

Not long after the air show I was asked by my counselor what I felt I needed most in order to deal with PTSD, I told her, "I need a break from being a people-helper. I need to not give out all the time." There were many times when I had to leave my personal counseling session, only to go back to my chapel office and have individuals and couples come to me for counseling. That made it impossible for me to fully open up in my personal counseling sessions. I always had to box up my stuff and be ready to focus on the other person/people's issues. Because of that, my counseling was, at best, a gasp of air to a man drowning. My repeated requests to be temporarily relieved of counseling duties were denied. "Everyone has to pull their own weight," my boss told me. Although I was able to keep my issues from coming up and staying up when I was counseling other people, that effort had a growing cost on me. I was heading toward a cliff and saw no way to stop.

Because of the traumatic events following Hurricane Katrina, Terri also began to struggle. When she sought out counseling help in Florida, she was diagnosed with PTSD, as well. We were both struggling for our lives.

In the midst of my struggles, we received the joyous news that Terri was pregnant with our fourth child. We eagerly and anxiously looked forward to that day. Although we were both wanting another child, we both were very anxious about caring for a newborn baby as we continued to struggle with our own heavy weights. Somehow, we would have to find the strength.

Stephen's birth came with excitement. We came home exhausted from the hospital, our cups overflowing with joy and still unresolved sorrows. Pressure was building in me. I was feeling more and more like a failure. Although I had dealt with the challenges of a newborn three times before, I had never had to do it while struggling for my survival with PTSD. I underestimated how weak I was and how strong PTSD was in me. I would soon pay for that underestimation.

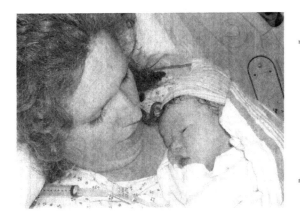

The joy of Stephen's birth and of his beautiful mom!

Only five days after witnessing the miracle of the birth of my son, I felt my world come crashing down around me. The final crack came from an argument with my wife. In the context of all that was swirling in my head and heart, what began as a 'simple' argument between us exploded into an indictment against my fundamental worth as a person. As I sat on the living room couch, I felt like a complete failure in all areas of my life. I felt overwhelmed, with no way out.

The wounding words from my struggles came flooding in. "Good chaplains give help... They don't need help..." I was sinking to the depths with my feet seemingly in concrete!

In my pain and despair, I yelled at my wife, "Maybe you and the kids would be better off if I weren't around anymore!" With that, I ran into my closet, got my shotgun and loaded a round. With tears of anguish pouring down my face, a part of me was saying "End it!" and a part was saying "This can't be the answer!" As I stood there in the closet for what seemed like hours, balancing between life and death, my mother came up behind me, crying and pleading with me not to end my life. Thoughts of my children in the next rooms raced through my head. I wanted to be there to walk my daughters down the aisle when they got married. I wanted to see my sons teaching their sons to play baseball.

A battle raged within me!

This was not the real answer! This could not be the answer! "God, help!!!" I cried out and slumped to the ground.

I lay the shotgun down and began walking out of the closet and through the master bedroom, with my mother right behind me. I had to find a better way to deal with what was going on.

As soon as I entered the bedroom, there they were!

They were standing in the doorway with their guns aimed at me!

7

DESPAIR WITH NO SHOE STRINGS

I immediately raised my hands as two Sheriff's Deputies ordered me to slowly walk towards them. We walked out to the living room, where they searched me for weapons and I sat down. Unbeknownst to me, when I said what I did to Terri and went to the closet, Terri was terrified and called 911. Four or five deputies were responding to Terri's desperate call for help for me.

As we sat there, I began to pour out the best explanation I could of what was happening. When one deputy went into the closet and found the loaded shotgun, they decided that I should be taken to a crisis center. All the deputies left, except for one. He would be the one to take me. I kissed my terrified children goodbye, not knowing what my future held. I was spiraling downward even more. I was taken to a crisis center in Tampa.

The deputy walked me into the intake area and I sat down in a room of fifteen to twenty people, all waiting for intake. Within a few minutes, I was called into a small room. As part of the intake process and a precaution, I was asked to take my shoe strings off and give them to the worker. As I pulled my shoe strings out of the shoes, I kept thinking. "How did I get here? This can't be happening to me! I've visited military personnel in places like this before. I visit here, I shouldn't be staying here!" I was sent back to the waiting area, each flopping step reminding me that my life had forever changed.

After a process of about ten hours and in the early morning hours, I was taken to the ward. Exhausted, I fell into the bed. Just before I fell asleep, I noticed a crisis center worker in a chair at the end of my bed. He was on suicide watch for me. Again I thought, "This can't be happening to me!" But it was.

After waking up later that morning, I got up to begin to try to make some sense of what I could not the night before. I met with a case worker and had the process and rules explained to me. The ramifications of what I had done and what was happening to me pressed down on me like a vice, squeezing hope out of me. Again I cried, "God, I need your help!" I didn't hear any audible voice in the storm, but I felt my hand was in His hand. Somehow, God would help me.

At the appointed lunch time, I and my fellow 'patients' were led to the dining area. We got our meals and sat to eat. I sat down at a table with a man quietly eating. Various conversations were going on around the small dining area. The topics were varied, many bordering on the bizarre. I was again reminded that this was a place where the mentally hurt and broken were. "But I shouldn't be here" I thought. But I <u>was</u> there.

After a few minutes, an argument at a nearby table grew louder. It soon had the attention of the whole dining room. One of the men arguing loudly shouted, "What, did one of the voices in your head tell you that?" At that, my quiet table companion spoke up. "Hey, that's not funny. Some of us really struggle with those voices in our head!" At that, the room grew quiet. I looked at this man sitting across the small table from me and saw him in a new light. As I sat there, I felt God open my eyes to a reality. This was a broken man, and so was I. Our brokenness was different, but we were both broken, nonetheless. I was not so different from him. We were broken and in need of wholeness and the Grace of God. For the first time since coming in to this place, I felt that God could use my brokenness to help others. I don't remember that man's name, but God used him to teach me something incredibly important about all of us as humans. We are all broken in one way or another. We all need God's healing.

For the next twenty four hours before I was released, I began to see opportunities to receive God's Grace, as well as to give it to my fellow sojourners. Something was changing in me. My healing had begun.

Because I was still on leave for the birth of my son, I decided not to call into work and tell them about what was happening. I greatly feared what Chaplain Ortiz would do to me if he knew about this. Surely this would 'prove' to him what a failure I was. I wanted help and wanted to tell my superiors outside the chapel. However, because of a confusing chain of command, I was not sure who was next in my chain of command outside the chapel. Was it the Wing Commander, the Mission Support Squadron Commander, or the Director of Wing Staff? Each had certain unknown responsibilities for me. This was not something that I wanted to call around about and tell more people than necessary. I also knew that there was no way to keep this from the military. The "right" people would find out. I just could not be the one to tell them at that time.

Our living room in a more peaceful time.
It was here, on May 5th, that I sat with Sheriff's
Deputies before being taken to the crisis center.

8

THE DREADED CALL CAME

After coming home, I tried to pick up the pieces. I went back to work and continued on as before. Each day I feared would be the day that what had happened would be discovered by the base and my career would be over. I met with my counselor and told her what had happened. We began to work more intently on the PTSD and Major Depression. I was even sent by the chapel and Sexual Assault Response Coordinator to a sexual assault response conference in Tampa. Several of the courses dealt with the PTSD so often associated with sexual assault. It was both healing and difficult to sit and listen as I was dealing with the same types of things myself. After coming back to work from the week-long conference, although I was still struggling with so much, I thought things were returning to 'normal.' That new 'normal' was short-lived.

On June 5th, 2007, I was off work for two days and working around the house. I got a call from Chaplain Ortiz telling me that I needed to report with him to the commander's office in an hour. I quickly got cleaned up and dressed and headed to the base. I stopped by Chaplain Ortiz's office and we walked to the building next to the chapel, where the commander's office was located. I asked Chaplain Ortiz if he knew what the meeting was about. He told me we would just have to wait and see. As a member of many commander's senior staffs, I had been called to commander's offices many times before. It did not register with me that this would be about me.

When I walked into the commander's office, I saw the First Sergeant already in there. I knew then that this was no ordinary meeting. As we sat down, the commander handed me a letter. With my hands trembling, I took it and read it. It stated that, because of the events of 5 May 2007 and my being taken to a crisis center for suicidal ideation, he was removing my security clearance, removing me from duty at the chapel and ordering a Commander Directed Mental Health Evaluation be given to me. May 5th had finally caught up with me! I signed for receipt of the letter and was permitted to go home for the rest of the day and the next. I was to report on 7 June to the base Life Skills Support Center to conduct the Evaluation. Some of my worst fears seemed to be realized! I felt my career was coming to an end.

I went home and told Terri what was happening. With both of us crying, we prayed and tried to let God intervene in the situation. Our faith told us that God heard our prayers, but we didn't feel like He did. We tried to occupy ourselves that evening, to keep from thinking of what we thought would be the impending doom to start on 7 June. I remember crying out in prayer that night the words from Psalm 22:1 that Jesus Himself had prayed while on the cross of Calvary, "My God, my God, why have you forsaken me?"

SECTION 2:

SURRENDER TO GOD!

The tragedy of life is what dies inside a man while he lives.
Albert Schweitzer

Take my yoke upon you and learn from me, for I am gentle and humble in heart, and you will find rest for your souls.
(Matthew 11:29)

Without holiness no one will see the Lord. (Hebrews 12:14)

I have come that you may have life, and have it to the full.
Jesus Christ (John 10:10)

An Unlikely Place to Meet With
The God of the Whole Universe?

*God will meet you right where you are, even in your
front yard while you mow the grass!*

9

THEN GOD WAS THERE!

I got up the next morning and decided to do yard work to occupy my mind. I felt as if the weight of the world were again pressing down on me. I knew that suicide was not the answer. I knew that somehow God would be with us through this time, as He had so many times before. I just didn't know how close God would be to me this time.

About mid-morning, I was mowing the front yard. The mowing had allowed me to calm my mind some. I didn't know what the next day would hold, but I was enjoying the low stress job of cutting grass. And then it happened!

Right there in the middle of my front yard, God answered my cries! God showed up!

As I was pushing the mower, I became overwhelmed by the Presence of God. I released the mower and fell to my knees. I was on holy ground!

Over the next hour, or two, or twenty (I could not tell), God spoke to me and ministered His Grace to my soul. God spoke many things to me that day, some of which He said was intended only for me. Some He told me to share with others. I will forever be grateful for those Words and the Grace they imparted. They changed my life forever!

In my spirit, God brought to my mind 2 Timothy 1:12 "Yet I am not ashamed, because I know whom I have believed, and am convinced that he is able to guard what I have entrusted to him for that day." I had known that verse for most of my life. I had memorized it years before. Yet I had not 'known' the truth of that verse until that day. As the truth of Paul's faith in Christ illustrated in that verse began to settle into my soul, the Holy Spirit brought to my mind the verse in the context which Paul wrote it to young Timothy. He brought me back to verse 8 of the chapter and brought the whole paragraph to my mind.

8 So do not be ashamed to testify about our Lord, or ashamed of me his prisoner. But join with me in suffering for the gospel, by the power of God, 9 who has saved us and called us to a holy life—not because of anything we have done but because of his own purpose and grace. This grace was given us in Christ Jesus before the beginning of time, 10 but it has now been revealed through the appearing of our Savior, Christ Jesus, who has destroyed death and has brought life and immortality to light through the gospel. 11 And of this gospel I was appointed a herald and an apostle and a teacher. 12 That is why I am suffering as I am. Yet I am not ashamed, because I know whom I have believed, and am convinced that he is able to guard what I have entrusted to him for that day.

With those verses fresh on my mind and heart, I understood that Paul suffered all that he did because of his calling by Jesus to proclaim the Gospel! It was not because of sin in his life. It was because he was faithful to that calling. God reminded me of the words of Jesus; that we are not greater than He is. If he suffered, so would we who follow Him. Paul was suffering, but was not ashamed of his suffering. He knew there was some One greater at work in him. He knew that he could trust that One with his life, because, as Jesus said, if he would try to save his life, he would lose it, but if he lost his life for Christ's sake, he would gain life.

God spoke to me that morning, right there in my front yard, with cars driving by. He said, "John, you are suffering because I called you. The traumas of war and Katrina and the betrayal of trust only came because you answered my call on your life to share My Love with people. You are not greater than Jesus. He suffered and you are too. You have entrusted Me with your life and I have not left you, nor will I ever. I will reward you for your faithfulness. I love you John." My heart nearly burst with joy! The clouds of doubt and depression that had hung over me for years were gone in an instant and the warming sunlight of God's Love and Presence shined down on me! He had not forsaken me!

I would like to tell you that every cloud in my sky was taken away that day. I would like to tell you that everything was great from that time forward. But that would not be the truth. There was still great clouds of adversity that I would face.

But the difference was that, after that day, I knew I was not alone in the struggle. Psalm 23:4 says "Even though I walk through the valley of the shadow of death, I will fear no evil, for you are with me; your rod and your staff, they comfort me." On June 6, 2007, I knew God was with me, even though I was still in the valley of the shadow of death.

If you're in the middle of a storm right now, God wants to be with you. Call out to Him. He may take all the clouds away at once. He may take them away over time. Or He may touch you with His rod and staff, letting you know you are not alone.

10

GOD IN THE STORM WITH YOU

I went to the appointment the next day for the evaluation with a new sense of hope and strength. The written results of the evaluation would not be completed for a week or more. During that time, my commander temporarily reassigned me to work with the Security Forces Squadron. He told me he wanted to give me the break from being responsible to counsel others, while they tried to figure out what was happening with me. I was pastoring the Gospel Service at the time. He also temporarily relieved me of the service. While I was with them, the commander and Chaplain Ortiz discussed whether to prohibit me from attending the Gospel Service. Although Chaplain Ortiz saw no problem with prohibiting me, the commander saw the larger ramifications of doing so. To specifically limit where I could worship would have unlawfully hindered my free exercise of my religion. This was the very freedom that chaplains are sworn to protect. The commander decided that I could attend, but not lead the service.

As I entered the sanctuary that Sunday, I was surprised to open the bulletin and see every reference to me, as the pastor, taken out. In its place was Chaplain Ortiz's name. Chaplain Ortiz led the service and made no mention of me during the whole service either. His common form of address for the congregation of "My Beloved" just did not seem to ring true to me that morning.

The completed evaluation was given to my commander a week later and revealed what I had already explained. I was suffering from PTSD and Major Depression, but was showing positive progress. The evaluation recommended that I should continue on active duty. My commander accepted the report, returned me to duty and sought to reinstate my security clearance.[††]

[††] What should have taken only a matter of a few weeks ended up taking more than a year. According to emails I received from several sources, the Air Force was not prepared to deal with issues raised by a chaplain struggling with PTSD. My reinstatement paperwork was stalled because no one wanted to be the one to make the decision on that issue. Fortunately, within a matter of a few weeks of my US Senator pressing for a decision, the Air Force made the decision to reinstate my security clearance, allowing me to continue in service to my country for a time.

Within a few weeks of returning to work at the chapel, Chaplain Ortiz sat me down and gave me paperwork stating that he was giving me a Referral Officer Performance Report. It would have been a career ending report. As I read over the report, it had numerous factual inaccuracies, as well as false, egregious and unsubstantiated statements about me. I looked Chaplain Ortiz in the eyes and said, "Are you trying to end my career?" He simply looked at me and said, "Sign the paper." I signed for receipt of the report and left to prepare my rebuttal. The report and my rebuttal would go to the Wing Chaplain for a decision of whether or not the Referral report was warranted. Unfortunately, the Wing Chaplain had just left the base for a new assignment. Because the new Wing Chaplain would not arrive for a month, I would have to track down the Wing Chaplain who had just left and present the rebuttal to him. I was in an all-out fight for my professional life.

I sat in my office and compiled a twenty page rebuttal. I addressed every statement made in the report. I included emails and written documents showing the truth about the situation and demonstrating the bias against me as the motivation for the report. I presented the information and documentation to the lawyer at the Area Defense Counsel on base. He felt the report was totally unjustified and was appalled at what my documentation showed about how I was treated by Chaplain Ortiz. He suggested I also take my documentation to the Inspector General (IG) and Military Equal Opportunity (MEO) offices on base. The battle lines widened for me.

I tracked down and submitted my rebuttal to the previous Wing Chaplain. As I waited for his response, I turned my attention to the IG and MEO offices. I provided copies of my documentation and explained everything that had gone on over the previous year. After hearing me out, leaders of both offices said they would look into my concerns and get back with me. I had to wait to hear my fate, again.

While waiting on an answer from the IG and MEO offices, I received a one line email from my previous Wing Chaplain. It simply stated, "The Referral OPR is being discontinued because of lack of documentation." Chaplain Ortiz was being told to rewrite the report! I had won one round in my battle for survival!

The following week I was called over to the IG office. What the base IG told me hit me like a ton of bricks. She said that, after reviewing all the documentation and conferring with the MEO chief, although my documentation did show discrimination against me, I was not part of a 'protected class.' The discrimination was not because of my race, gender, religion, or any other classification contained in the current regulations. I was discriminated against because I had received mental health help. The discrimination was not because my condition led me to poor performance. The issue shown by my documentation was the very fact that I received mental health help. I was a victim of the very real stigma against getting mental health help in the military. When the IG told me that the current rules said there was nothing wrong with the way I was treated, something welled up inside of me. I remember telling the IG, "Then the rules will have to be changed! If this is the way a chaplain and a captain is treated, why would an Airman with one stripe on his arm, who's been driving convoys in Iraq or Afghanistan and seen his buddies blown up near him, ask for help. I have more resources than he does. Who's going to fight for him?

I will!"

I had fought off Chaplain Ortiz's overt attempts to end my career and now had a mission to change the rules that allowed the treatment I had received and help those men and women in uniform that I had been called to serve. I had no idea how I would do that, but I knew I needed to do what I could.

About a month after getting the email about the end of the Referral report and that the IG and MEO offices could do nothing for me, my new Wing Chaplain arrived on base. During our initial meeting, he asked me how things had been going for me, a common question for introductions. So I told him.

As I opened up the stack of documentation that I had brought with me, I shared with him my experiences of the past year, especially the previous couple months. I told him that I felt like I could not get a fair chance if I continued to be supervised by Chaplain Ortiz. For all the reasons I laid out, I requested a formal Change of Reporting Official away from Chaplain Ortiz. That would take away Chaplain Ortiz's ability to continue to harm me and my career. He listened intently and caringly. He didn't seem to take either my or Chaplain Ortiz's side. He said he would look into it. I believed him and left his office feeling like I actually had an objective chance to serve. I welcomed the fresh air and awaited his decision.

That decision came within a month. After talking with the Wing Commander and others, he made the decision to grant my request for Change of Reporting Official, taking me out from under Chaplain Ortiz and placing me directly under him, instead. Although that action would generate a final performance report from Chaplain Ortiz, I felt my Wing Chaplain would ensure that it did not contain the overt, career ending bias shown before. In the end, both the rewritten OPR and the one generated by the change in bosses were poorly written, not something that could force a re-write. At least they were done and I could move on...

But my tank was on empty. Although I did feel God's presence with me, I was physically and mentally exhausted. I asked my counselor about being sent to a pastoral counseling retreat out of the area, where I could get some intensive counseling without my normal responsibilities. Because much of my trauma involved caring for other people as a chaplain, I felt I needed a Christian counseling retreat especially for pastors. She thought that may be exactly what I needed. I searched for the right program. I found one quickly and with my counselor's written recommendation, I started the process to get approval from Tricare (the military medical insurance). Even with my counselor and primary care doctor's recommendation, my request was denied. "We don't do things like that" was the answer that came back.

I found another program that had an excellent reputation for helping people like me. It was even cheaper than the first one. Again it was denied.

A third time I searched and found an excellent program, especially for pastors in crisis. This one was even free to me! It was called the Pastors Retreat Network, with a location in Texas. Because of the extremely generous support of donors, they were able to offer retreats free to pastors in crisis. We just had to pay our way to get there.

Again with the recommendation of my counselor and primary care doctor, I presented this retreat proposal to Tricare, just asking to have my travel expenses paid and to be put on Permissive Temporary Duty orders. Surely they would approve this one?

But they didn't. "We've never done something like that" was the final answer.

Again I felt cornered, with despair pressing down on me. But this time, I did something different. I called my Ecclesiastical Endorser, Chaplain Scott McChrystal.‡‡ Although I felt very ashamed of myself and still very unsure of whom I could trust, I needed to ask for his help. I told

---

‡‡ All military chaplains must be endorsed by a religious body recognized by the Department of Defense. Without that endorsement, the chaplain cannot serve in the military. That endorsement means that the chaplain answers to two organizations. As a commissioned officer in the military, he or she is accountable to the military. As an ordained, endorsed clergy, he or she is accountable to their endorsing agency. The head of the endorsing agency was usually known as our Endorser. In my denomination, the Assemblies of God, our Endorsers have always been retired chaplains with incredible depths of experience.

him all that had happened, as well as my denied requests for a counseling retreat.

With the compassionate heart of a pastor and the drive and intensity of the Army Colonel that he was, he listened, counseled, and committed to help in any way he could. I was not alone in the fight.

Before long, Chaplain McChrystal called me and told me that the Assemblies of God Chaplaincy Department was going to send Terri and me to the counseling retreat! As I hung up the phone, I couldn't adequately put into words what I felt. The best I can do is to describe it with a word picture from my diving accident of a few years before.

Just before panic had gripped me, I hit the surface of the water. As I shot out of the water and gasped for air, the air tasted and smelled different then it had before I went on the dive. As the air came into my lungs, I remember thinking and feeling, "I'm going to live!" Although I still had the hard work of swimming to safety of the reef, I knew I would make it. I had air to breathe.

As Terri and I prepared ourselves and the kids to head to Texas, where we would drop the three older kids with grandparents before driving to the retreat, I was hoping and praying for rest and healing. Terri and I needed physical, emotional and spiritual air.

And that is what we got. The one week retreat gave Terri and me a chance to rest, sleep, pray, and talk. We, individually and as a couple, felt the comfort of the rod and staff of the Good Shepherd that Psalm 23 talks about. Though we knew there was still a fight ahead of me when we got back home to the base, we left recharged, with our hope renewed.

While I waited to hear the fate of my OPR and career, Chaplain McChrystal dedicated our new baby to God in front of the military chaplains of my denomination.

Not long after I got back, Chaplain Ortiz received orders for an excellent next assignment and moved a few months later. (Somehow it just did not sit well with me that he was given a good assignment after what he had done and tried to do to me. However, I decided to trust that the God of all the universe would do what is right.) My boss told me that I would be transferred back under the new Senior Protestant Chaplain when he arrived. In a few months, my new boss arrived on the base. To say I was nervous about meeting him would be like saying survivors of the Titanic were a little skittish about ice and water. I was terrified of what he might do, but I was also holding on to the hope that he was different.

After talking with him only a few minutes, I knew he was different. As Chaplain Bill Coker compassionately listened to me, I felt the Hope of God's Grace. God had sent him to me and I would receive him. He was and is a true Man of God. Great healing from God came through him. I will be forever grateful to God and my Brother Bill, who remains a dear friend to this day.

As the months marched on, my mental and emotional healing continued, even as my physical health got worse. Although God lifted the dark clouds on June 6, 2007, the rest of my mental and emotional healing would take years. In

December 2008, I went into the Emergency Room with severe abdominal pain. After testing, I was diagnosed with severe Diverticulitis and admitted to the hospital. I spent the next four days on several intravenous antibiotics, being released right before Christmas. Over the next several months, I endured many medical tests to find out what was happening with me. The specialists concluded that I had no risk factors and that the episode was unexplained. One doctor simply said, "We'll just have to watch and see what happens."

Several months later, I was riding the county bus home from base. The afternoon ride was often a quiet ride. Everyone was tired from the long day and we enjoyed letting someone else drive while we snoozed, read, or listened to music. The ride seemed no different than the countless ones I had taken before. But this one would change my life.

I sat quietly looking out the window. So many things were going through my mind. I just chose to shut them all out and to sit in silence. About twenty minutes into the thirty minute drive, it happened.

I "heard" the voice of God in my spirit. He simply said, "John, nothing you could do would make Me love you more and nothing you could do would make Me love you less. I love you because I created you and put my Image in you. I have reached out and showed you my love and it will not change."

With those few words my heart and mind were opened. I realized that the source of my struggles really came from my trying to be good enough to be loved and accepted, by God and by other people. When other people told me that I did not measure up to them, I had transferred that rejection to my relationship with God. Without realizing it, I believed that I had to show God that I was worth loving. I had to show Him that I was a good man, a good husband, a good father, and a good minister. And I had interpreted "good" to really mean "perfect." When I encountered circumstances of such magnitude that I, and anyone else, was wholly inadequate to meet, I believed that I failed and proved that I was not worth loving.

In those few short minutes on that bus, God opened my eyes to my worth in Him. I stepped off the bus with tears streaming down my cheeks. But these were tears of joy. God loves me and nothing could change that. Words that kept going over and over in my head and heart were "In Christ Alone!" My fundamental worth and value as a human being were to be found in Christ alone!

My mind flashed back to 1993, shortly after I started studying to become a pastor. I was at a concert where

Christian artist Michael English sang one of my favorite songs, entitled "In Christ Alone." The lyrics that came flooding like sunlight through parting rain clouds were, "My source of strength, my source of hope, is Christ alone."

From that day on, I serve God, not out of a desire to make Him love me more, or fear that He will love me less. I serve Him out of gratitude for who He is and what He has already done for me.

As you read this, know that God does not love me more than He loves you. He has demonstrated His love for you by sending His One and Only Son, Jesus Christ and wants to wrap His arms of love around you and bring you close.

Your fundamental value is in Christ alone and no power on earth or in Hell can take that away!

*Again showing that He was at work in my life, God
gave me the privilege of baptizing my daughter,
Lydia, in water at the base chapel!
(Little brother Tim is curious of what's going on)*

11

WHEN GOD OPENS A DOOR, STEP IN

I continued to serve and look for the way God would open up the doors for the Air Force's rules to change. I still had no idea how He would do it. In fact, in the early spring of 2009, Terri and I sat with Chaplain McChrystal and his wife in our living room and shared, "I feel like there's just one more thing that needs to happen to close this chapter of my life. The rules of the Air Force must be changed to prevent this from happening again." I couldn't have known that three weeks later I would be in Washington D.C. to do just that!

While at a meeting on base a week later, the chairwoman reported that the Air Force was convening a group in Washington of about three hundred people from around the Air Force to tell the Air Force how it could better take care of its people. The group was the first annual "Caring for People Forum." Two people from our base were invited to attend. When the group voted, the chairwoman and I were selected. I was on my way to changing the rules!

I arrived with great anticipation and anxiety. I had a story to tell and change needed to come. Over the course of the week both would happen.

The group was broken down into smaller and smaller groups, until each person was a part of a group of four or five people. Each small group was to come up with two or three ideas of how the Air Force could better take care of people. Those ideas would be presented to the next larger group, of five or six smaller groups combined. After all ideas were presented to that group, the larger group would vote on which ones to send to the next level up, until the final ones would be presented to Generals and other senior Air Force and Department of Defense personnel.

In my small group, I told them about "this Airman I know" and shared my story briefly. I pointed out what the rules currently said and what rules I felt needed to be changed in order to encourage people to get help who needed it. Fortunately, my proposal was adopted by each level, eventually being presented to the senior leaders at the end of the conference. In accepting the final recommendations, the Lieutenant General who convened the forum said he would have each one worked on starting the following week. I set out to change the Air Force, and now it looked like it would happen!

*A view of the US Capital on my trip to change the
Air Force...*

I returned to my base and continued serving, thankful to have had any part in helping bring positive change. God was blessing my efforts to help marriages and families on base. I felt I was truly making a difference in people's lives. Then, a couple short months after returning from Washington, the email hit my inbox.

I opened the email with a file attached. The file was a newly signed Department of Defense Instruction (DoDI), which carry the weight of law for military members. It was not unusual to get notice of new AFIs and DoDIs. That happened regularly. However, this one was different. This was DoDI 6490.06, dealing with the subject "Counseling Services for DoD Military, Guard and Reserve, Certain Affiliated Personnel, and Their Family Members." As I read through the document, I saw it was an answer to the proposal I took to Washington just a couple short months before! For the first time, the Department of Defense put into writing rules to:

a. Promote a culture that encourages delivery and receipt of counseling.

b. Eliminate barriers to and the negative stigma associated with seeking counseling support

c. Empower leaders to advocate for those in their charge to receive counseling.

d. Provide easy access to a continuum of counseling support to include prevention, early intervention, and treatment to enhance coping and build resilience.

e. View counseling support as a force multiplier enhancing military and family readiness.

I had set out to change the Air Force, but God had allowed me to be a small part of changing the Department of Defense! This was a large first step toward preventing what was done to me from being done to others!

118

This new requirement was even referenced in Recommendation 5.3 of the January 2010 "Protecting the Force: Lessons from Fort Hood" Report of the DoD Independent Review of the Fort Hood shooting. The third recommendation of 5.3 was to "Review the requirement of the Department of Defense to de-stigmatize healthcare providers who seek treatment for stress."[§§]

The Report defined "caregivers" to include "healthcare providers...chaplains, medics, corpsmen, and counselors."[***] Furthermore, Finding 5.2 recognized that, even as late as the end of 2009, "The Department of Defense does not have comprehensive policies that recognize, define, integrate, and synchronize monitoring and intervention efforts to assess and build healthcare provider readiness." Recommendation 5.2 stated the need to "Create a body of policies that...addresses individual assessment, fatigue prevention, non-retribution, and reduced stigma for those seeking care, and appropriate procedures for supporting clinical practice during healthcare provider recovery."[†††]

[§§] DoD Independent Review Panel, "Protecting the Force: Lessons from Fort Hood," 2010, 53.
[***] Ibid, 49.
[†††] Ibid, 52.

My prayer and continuing desire is to continue to fight for all wounded warriors, but especially those who are also caregivers.

With God's help, one person can make a difference!

12

THE ROAD IS FILLED WITH POTHOLES

Many times the road to recovery and wholeness is smooth from the point a decision to seek help is made. Most of the time it's not. Most of the time, the road to healing has many potholes. Those potholes don't mean you're off the road to wholeness, just that you live in a fallen, imperfect world. Although I have seen God do many incredible things, I, too, was a part of the majority.

As best as I could remember, since I began to struggle with PTSD, I had not been able to sleep well. The norm was for me to wake up feeling like I had not slept. As I was healing from PTSD, my doctors and I expected that I would sleep better. Unfortunately, that was not happening. Finally, four months after reading the new DoDI, I was tested and diagnosed with Sleep Apnea. It was severe enough to need a breathing machine. "After all I've been through, would this end my military career," I wondered.

Then, in November, 2009, I received word that I would receive orders to move to become the new Senior Protestant Chaplain at Malmstrom Air Force Base, in Great Falls, Montana! As a captain who had not yet met his promotion board for Major, it was a bit unusual to be put in such position. I was excited about the possibilities of a fresh start and of being promoted to Major. The road seemed to be getting smoother.

In March 2010, my family and I packed up our van and drove from Tampa, Florida to Great Falls, Montana to start the next chapter of our lives, and unbeknownst to us at the time, the final chapter of our military life. After an eight day journey across country, we arrived in Great Falls and checked into our temporary housing. After signing into the base, we went hunting for a house to live in.

The evening of the second day there, I began to feel the same pains I had felt before I was hospitalized before Christmas 2008. I drove myself to the Emergency Room and prayed. After testing, I was again diagnosed with Diverticulitis. However, because I had caught it earlier than before, I was able to take strong oral antibiotics and be able to stay at 'home' instead of the hospital. After a few days, I began to feel better. My doctor at the base clinic again referred me to a specialist to see why this had happened again. After further testing, the specialist said that if I had any more episodes, we would have to consider surgery to remove a portion of my colon. Again I felt as if a ton of bricks were dropped on me. "Would this end my military career?" I feared.

Over the next four months, I had three more episodes of infection, ultimately leading me to sit down with a surgeon to discuss removing a portion of my colon. As I sat in the office of the surgeon, I heard him talking of the risks of the surgery. If I didn't have the surgery, I ran the risk of possibly life threatening episodes in the future. If all went well with the surgery, I may have no further complications from it. If things didn't go well, I may die or have major, life altering results. "This can't be happening to me!" I bemoaned to myself.

After talking with Terri and praying, I decided to have the surgery. The surgery was scheduled for the end of August, two weeks before I was scheduled to travel to South Carolina for my Senior Protestant Chaplain's training course at the Chaplain Corps College. The surgeon felt that I would be recovered enough to travel, so we went ahead.

The surgery went well. I had more than a foot of my colon removed. After three days recovering in the hospital, I was sent home for two weeks of rest and recovery.

At the end of those two weeks, I went back to the surgeon and was cleared by him to fly to South Carolina for the class. Because of my overall health, he decided not to put me on blood thinners following surgery. It was another decision that changed the course of my life.

13

THE DAY I ALMOST DIED, AGAIN

On September 12, 2010 I flew to Columbia, South Carolina from Great Falls, Montana. Although I was in pain, I was able to make it through the first day of class. The night was a different matter. Pain began to increase as I finished eating and prepared for bed. I began to have sharp, stabbing pains in my side and back. As the night wore on, the pain increased. I was having trouble breathing, only able to take very short breaths. About two in the morning, I knew something was very wrong with me. I dialed 911 and prayed.

The ambulance soon arrived and rushed me to Providence Hospital Northeast. Not long after I arrived, they gave me a couple shots of pain killers. The pain began to subside as they took an x-ray to determine the cause. When nothing showed on the x-ray, the doctor told me, "We don't know what's wrong with you, but, since the pain has subsided, we're going to send you home." With that, I was discharged and sent back to the base. It was then about seven in the morning.

I was told to stay in my quarters and rest for the day, which I gladly did. However, as the pain killing shots wore off in a few hours, the pain began coming back. By late afternoon, the pain was back with a vengeance. I called a classmate and asked him to take me to the medical clinic on post. When I explained my symptoms and my experience at the ER earlier that morning, they ran some basic tests (which the ER that morning had failed to do). Within a few minutes, I went from having one technician in my ER room, to having eight to ten doctors, nurses and technicians! Each was almost stumbling over the other as they tried to get me on pure oxygen and get me to sign paperwork to have me taken by ambulance to a downtown hospital. They could not find an adult mask, so in their haste to get me on oxygen, they put a small pediatric mask on me. It only covered my nose! The tests had all come back indicating the possibility of pulmonary emboli; blood clots in my lungs. That was more than they were equipped to deal with, so again I was in the back of an ambulance being rushed back to the same hospital I was at that morning.

As I looked out the back of the ambulance, seeing the red and blue lights reflect off the windshields of cars pulling out of the way to let us through, fear and panic began to well up within me. Every short breath brought more pain than I had ever experienced. Was I dying? I began to feel sadness. Thoughts of my daughters' weddings without me walking down the aisle flashed before my eyes. My sons growing up without me and my wife weeping at my funeral all swirled around my head. Even as my faith told me I would see them all again in Heaven, I mourned not being with them any more on Earth. Panic began to cloud my thoughts. I remember thinking, "John, if you panic, you're going to die! Pray!"

But what do you pray to get the attention of the God of the whole universe that would convince Him to save your life? Just like when I sat in the back of the church while my baby son, Timothy, lay in the hospital dying, I wanted to pray a "big" prayer. But nothing came to me. I could "only" pray, "God, help me!"

But that was enough.

In that moment, I felt the presence of God come in that ambulance. I felt what I've come to know was the Grace of God coming upon me and the Holy Spirit helping me to pray. With the empowering Grace of God on me, I simply prayed over and over, "God, I trust you!" As I uttered those words from my soul, I felt the "peace of God which transcends all understanding" come over me. God didn't tell me I was going to live or die. I simply knew that I was in His Hands and that I trusted Him to take care of everything. In that moment, my faith and life were forever changed. Although the physical pain remained intense, the spiritual pain was replaced by peace. God was with me!

I arrived back at the same hospital I was at earlier that day. I was wheeled into the ER and passed off from the paramedics to the ER staff. As soon as the paramedics left, I overheard the ER nurse tell another worker, "Those base people overreact all the time." He, apparently, felt there was nothing serious happening with me.

I lay on the bed for what seemed like hours, waiting for someone to help me. I took out my cell phone to call Terri and tell her what was happening and saw it was almost dead. I had neglected to charge it when I got back to my room earlier. Because I didn't know how long it would last, I told her I would shut it off to save power for me to make outgoing calls. I asked her to call friends and family and have them pray. If she needed to get in touch with me, she would have to call the hospital. I hung up, not knowing if or when I would talk with her next.

The nurse told me to lay down, but every time I began to lay down, the pain spiked to unbearable. I asked for a pain killer like I had been given that morning. He refused to even bring it up to a doctor. (He still did not think there was anything serious happening with me.) He told me he was sending me for a CT scan and that I would have to lay down very still for several minutes. When I told him I could not, he wrote in my chart that I was "non-compliant" and left me in the ER room. About an hour later, a technician came in and got me for the CT scan. As she wheeled me into the room, I explained to her that I could not lay down because of the pain and that I had explained that to the nurse. She said she understood and turned around and brought me back to the ER room. After a couple hours and desperate pleas for help, I was given a shot for pain and spiral CT tests run. When the tests came back, they showed two pulmonary emboli in my right lung. (The nurse's attitude toward me changed completely. Was it compassion or fear of a malpractice lawsuit? There really was something physically wrong with me!) We now knew what I was up against. Now we turned to fighting for my survival. I was given shots of medication to begin dissipating the clots. I remember the nurse remarking under his breath to another nurse, "Hopefully we're in time."

I was admitted to the hospital and spent the next five days hospitalized, four at Providence and the fifth on post at the hospital. During the second day at the hospital, I was told that, because I had already missed three days of classes I was being dropped from the course and would have to re-take it at some time in the future. It was another blow. The doctors told me that I was "lucky to be alive." After further testing, it showed that the clots should have killed me. When I was released from the hospital, I was cleared to fly back to my base in Montana. I hoped for a more peaceful time when I got there. But that was not to happen.

After a couple more days to recover at home, I returned to work at the chapel. On the day I returned, I was called to the Vice Wing Commander's office. Knowing him to be a Christian and compassionate man, I thought he just wanted to express his concerns for my health. I wish that was all that it was.

When I arrived in his office, he asked me to sit down. He handed me a letter and told me that I had not been selected for Major at the promotion board that had met a few months earlier. My mind swooned and my heart sank as I heard, but could not believe, the words I was hearing. "Haven't I been through enough God?" I breathed in prayer. I left his office reeling and wondering, "Is this the end of my military career?"

But that was not to be the end of our trials. Two weeks later, to our heart-breaking surprise, Bubbles, our cat of fifteen years' health drastically declined in a matter of days, and she died. Holding her lifeless body, I cried out, "God, how much can one person endure??!!"

(Above) Bubbles on a happier day.
(Below) We said "Goodbye" to Bubbles

14

CRAWLING ON

Still reeling and mourning myself and trying to comfort my family at our beloved pet's death, I had to return to work. I was numb. I was physically, mentally and emotionally exhausted. I was desperately holding on to the hope of my faith in God. Somehow God would work all this out! I hoped and prayed.

The following week I had a follow up appointment with my base doctor to check on my recovery from the clots. Although I was making progress, it would be months yet before I would know the extent of the damage to my lungs. To add to my hurdles, she told me that regulations required that I go through a Medical Evaluation Board, to determine if I was still fit for duty and continued service in the military. The process would begin immediately and could be over in a matter of weeks, or could take many months. I could be returned to full duty, or I could be discharged from the service. I didn't think I could have gotten any lower, but I did. It seemed that my life was unraveling again. But this time, I was a different person. I didn't know how, but I knew I was going to make it through all this.

For the next six months, I went to work each day wondering if that would be the day the Medical Evaluation Board results would come back and my career would be over. The stresses of being in leadership at a nuclear missile base were intense. Over those six months, one of my good chaplains was discharged from the Air Force through a Reduction In Forces board. Two months after that, an Airman from our base committed suicide. Three weeks later, an officer from our base also committed suicide. I was appointed by the Wing Commander to both Suicide Review Panels. We were trying to determine what happened and how to prevent anything similar again. While I was on the Panels, another of my chaplains, still at his first active duty base, decided to separate from the Air Force. That would leave three chaplains to do the work of five, with me heavily involved with the investigations. The intensity of stress was overwhelming, but I had to go on. I sought help from a counselor off-base, so I would not allow myself back to where I had gone in Florida. No matter what happened, I would not go back!

After two months, the Suicide Review Panels completed and we made our reports to levels up the whole chain of command. Although my observations and feedback were corroborated by other panel members, they were not well received by leadership. I had done my duty faithfully, but it took a toll on my physically and mentally. I was beyond exhausted.

Then, in April 2010, I was back at Fort Jackson in Columbia, South Carolina for a course at the Chaplain Corps College. As I jogged the streets that I had traveled in ambulance only six months earlier, I had a profound sense of gratitude to God for saving my life then. I didn't know how any of what I was dealing with would end, but I knew God would take care of it. The class went well and I was soon sitting on the tarmac at the airport, about to leave for home. Just then, my phone rang and the call that began the end of my military career came.

It was the Physical Evaluation Board Liaison Officer (PEBLO) from my base. She said, "Chaplain VanderKaay, the Board results have come back and you're being medically retired."

15

THE RACE TO THE END OF A CAREER

That was news that I did not want to give my wife over the phone. I held it in until I got home that evening. We went out to dinner on a date that night. While we were eating, I said, "Terri, the medical board results have come back. I'm being medically retired." Even as I heard myself saying it, I couldn't believe it. Terri was in shock, too. After a couple minutes of silence, I held her hand and told her, with all the faith I could muster, "God is going to take care of us."

Terri and I went the next morning to the PEBLO's office. When everything was explained, I signed the results, starting the six week race to end my military career. Almost six weeks from the day I signed the paperwork, I had my last day of work in the military. What had been building for almost fifteen and a half years was ending in six weeks!

As soon as I got back to the chapel and informed my boss of my news, I had to start out processing and shutting down my career. It was a blur for the most part. After my last day at work, I had several weeks of permissive temporary duty time to find a new house and look for a job. It all happened so quickly that it really did not settle in until after I had left the military. My uniformed military journey had come to an end. That chapter of my life closed on July 23, 2011 and the next one started. As I moved on, I looked back and asked, "What do I do with these scars?"

16

WHEN OUR SCARS BECOME HOLY

Since medically retiring from the military, I have begun to understand many things about my experiences. I have had a lot of pain in my life, not unlike most people. I would love to say that God completely healed me of every physical and mental wound and that I no longer struggle with either. But that is not what has happened. I have scars, in my body and my mind. There are still times of struggle in both. I am regularly reminded of the prayer of the Apostle Paul for Jesus to remove the "thorn" in his flesh. Jesus certainly could have removed the thorn, but He did not. Instead, He gave His grace to strengthen Paul, with the thorn intact. The specific experiences we all have are unique, but pain is common to us all. Although there were many times when I could not imagine how anything good could come from what I was going through, I now see that good has come from them. But it's a different good than I would have imagined before it all began.

I have heard Romans 8:28 quoted my whole Christian life, most often in hospital rooms and funeral homes. "And we know that in all things God works for the good of those who love him, who have been called according to his purpose." While I certainly believed the words were true, I did not understand what they truly meant. I have come to understand them in a much more powerful way on this side of all that I've gone through.

The Apostle Paul was not telling the Christians in Rome that they had to look at everything, especially the difficult things they experienced, as something good. How could being beaten be good? How could being betrayed be good? How could having your shoestrings taken and spending time locked in a crisis center be good? They are not good! They are bad!

I've come to believe that what Paul was talking to the Roman believers about was not rejoicing when bad things happen, but rejoicing that, no matter what bad things happen, God can bring good from them. And there's a world of difference between the two. One leads to resentment of God and the other leads to peace from God. Which one will you choose?

The Apostle Paul was talking to Christians. He was talking to people who had already put their faith in Christ. That is the prerequisite Paul wrote about. For God to take even the bad things that happen to us and bring good from them, we must have put our trust in Him. Paul wasn't talking about just going to church. He was talking about knowing who Christ is and what He has done, repenting of our sins and accepting His gift of Salvation. When that happens, God's promise is that He will work everything we experience to our good. But does that 'good' mean smiles and roses? Not necessarily.

Most importantly, that 'good' is to fulfill God's highest purposes for each of our lives, to be in a close relationship with Him. To be in a close relationship with God requires holiness. The writer of Hebrews wrote in Hebrews 12:14 (NIV) "without holiness no one will see the Lord." Only four verses earlier, the writer recorded "God disciplines us for our good, in order that we may share in his holiness." God desires fellowship with us and has gone to incredible lengths to make it possible. When we love Him, He will bring about more of our holiness, allowing greater fellowship with Him to happen. God desires wholeness in us, physically, mentally, and spiritually, because of the joy it can bring. But He desires holiness in us even more, because it brings us closer to Him. It is then that our scars become holy. They can bring us closer to the absolutely holy God.

17

PAIN IN ISOLATION

We were all created for relationships. From the first chapter of Genesis, we see that God created each one of us with an undeniable need for relationships, first with Him, then with other people. Within every human being is this powerful ache for relationships. Think about punishment at high security prisons. When a convict serving a life sentence breaks a major rule, what is the worst punishment usually given to him? Is it not Solitary Confinement? As punishment, all relationships but the very minimal needed for survival are removed. There is pain in isolation.

The highest type of relationship is the truly intimate one, where one is wholly known and accepted. Before the Fall, Adam and Eve had that kind of relationship with God and each other. But when they allowed sin to enter them, that relationship was marred, at best.

The need for relationships like those in the Garden of Eden did not go away. They became impossible without God's help. And so Jesus Christ came and made a way for us to have those relationships.

Truly intimate relationships are built on Trust. When that trust is broken, there is great conflict within a person. Not only does the offense often hurt, but the isolation from the person who caused the harm hurts. There are often feelings of loss for what "could have been" in the relationship.

One of the most effective tools of Satan is to make humans believe that they are all alone, to counter how God created them. "Nobody understands." "Nobody cares." "I did this to myself and I deserve this." "I can't trust anyone."

PTSD, as well as many other major stresses and anxieties, drives a person toward isolation. Whether that drive is because of shame, or hurt, or fear of more hurt, it drives away from close relationships.

Although I did not understand it at the time I was going through most of my intense stress, I believe one of the decisions I made that helped change my life was to seek relationships instead of pulling away from them. I wanted to have relationships that I could trust. I wanted to be known and accepted. I truly believed that was what I was created for.

That is also where I was challenged the most. I had several types of relationships. I had those, especially my wife and a few others, who loved me and knew and accepted me. I had those who I always kept at arm's length, because trust had not been built up further, but could be with time and a little effort. And I also had those relationships where I gave trust to those who proved untrustworthy.

When I chose to trust the two chaplains above me with information of my struggles with PTSD, they proved untrustworthy in those areas. I felt betrayed, but, for quite a while, I also had to remain under their authority. Was I wrong to tell them about my struggles?

One of my mentors thought so.

Near the end of 2009, I was talking with a senior ranking chaplain who I had great respect for. We talked about what I had gone through, and how the two chaplains had taken what I entrusted to them and abused me with it. He looked at me and said, "John, if you hadn't told them that, this wouldn't have happened. You've learned that was not the wisest thing to do, right?"

Even as he said that, something just did not seem right about that. Was trusting them with the information about me the wrong thing because they betrayed that trust, or was trusting them the right thing, because of who they were supposed to be and that it was their betrayal of that trust that was wrong? I should have been able to trust religious leaders in authority over me and ask for appropriate help from them. I do not believe that was wrong. I believe they were wrong for the things they did, but I was not wrong for trusting them, based on what I knew about them at the time. Vulnerability is a part of the trust that makes intimate relationships possible.

I have come to understand what Jesus said to us in Matthew 5:44-45.

"But I tell you, love your enemies and pray for those who persecute you, 45 that you may be children of your Father in heaven. He causes his sun to rise on the evil and the good, and sends rain on the righteous and the unrighteous."

When we experience tragedy, heartache and trials, my faith as a Christian tells me the truth: that God isn't picking on me. Whether the trial is an attack of Satan, an unfortunate result of living in a sin-filled world, or a deliberate act of God, the outcome can all be the same. God can bring good from it.

However, it does require things of me. I learned that I am to love and pray for those who wrong me. I learned that the right to bring justice ultimately belongs only to God. He does indeed delegate some of that authority to human governments, as His representatives. To us, individually, as human beings, Jesus said in John 7:7, when speaking to the accusers of the woman caught in adultery, "Let any one of you who is without sin be the first to throw a stone."

I found it easier to work through the traumas of Iraq and Katrina than the trauma of being betrayed by one whom I should have been able to trust and be helped by. I have chosen to forgive Chaplain Ortiz because I desire a closer relationship with God. Although, as of the last time we communicated, Chaplain Ortiz felt he did no wrong and was right in how he treated me, I chose to forgive him. He did not deserve that forgiveness. But then, neither did I deserve the forgiveness or grace that God gave me. Forgiveness is an act of Grace. I was given it, so I will give it. But it did not come naturally to me.

18

FORGIVENESS ISN'T NATURAL

Through my experiences, I have come to understand the extreme importance of forgiveness in all relationships. I also learned that forgiveness is not the same as reconciliation. When a person breaks trust in a relationship, part of the relationship is broken.[‡‡‡] For the relationship to continue forward, the break must be repaired. That repair is called *reconciliation*. Reconciliation is repaired trust.

But there are two parts to reconciliation: Forgiveness and Repentance, or Genuine Apology. Forgiveness is the responsibility of the Offended. Repentance/Genuine Apology is the responsibility of the Offender. Both Forgiveness and Repentance/Genuine Apology are necessary for reconciliation to happen. If either is missing, reconciliation cannot happen.

I had a pretty good understanding about what Repentance/Genuine Apology was supposed to look like.

[‡‡‡] While I do believe that there are offenses that completely break all trust in a relationship, thankfully, they are much rarer than those that are not complete breaks of all trust.

That was the easier part for me. I recognized that I had done wrong things, to God and others. As a Christian who grew up in the church, I knew that I had to repent for my wrongs. I also knew that it was much easier to forgive someone who had genuinely repented and apologized. Where I struggled most was with the part of forgiving the unrepentant.

How important is forgiveness?

Jesus thought it important enough to mention it at some pretty important times. When His followers asked Jesus to teach them to pray, Jesus told them what we call "The Lord's Prayer." Right in the middle of the prayer, found in Matthew 6:8-13, are the words, "forgive us our debts, as we also have forgiven our debtors." Then, as soon as the prayer is finished, Jesus emphasized how important forgiveness is. Knowing the very thoughts of their hearts, Jesus looked at his followers and said, "[14]For if you forgive other people when they sin against you, your heavenly Father will also forgive you. [15]But if you do not forgive others their sins, your Father will not forgive your sins."

Forgiveness is a choice. Jesus made it clear that, for Christians, forgiveness is not an optional choice, it is a command! If I did not forgive Chaplain Ortiz and others who had wronged me, I would not be forgiven by God! "But God, how do I do that?" I often prayed. "This is not easy!"

147

The principles I learned about biblical forgiveness apply whether or not the Offender ever recognizes and repents of the offences. I believe biblical forgiveness fundamentally does not have anything to do with the Offender. It has to do with the Offended person and God. Many people misunderstand this.

Consider it this way...

If you have been wronged and you do not forgive, the Offender is not the one harmed the most. You are. In unforgiveness, you allow the Offender to continue to negatively affect your life. Forgiveness breaks the power of the Offender to continue harming you. Unforgiveness locks you into memories and pain of the past. Every time a memory of that person came up, you remember the offense or offenses. The pain comes right back. Forgiveness allows you to move forward in life, even if that is without the presence of the Offender.

If I did not forgive those who wronged me, they would continue to direct areas of my life in a negative direction. I would not let them do that!

As I wrestled with how to do that, God taught me a lesson through an ordinary occurrence, as Jesus so often did while He was here on earth. This lesson has stayed with me for years.

In November and December of 2008, I was on a temporary duty assignment in Alabama. While there, I was only a short drive from one of my good friends, Jim. Ever since our days in seminary, Jim, an Army chaplain, and I have seldom let an opportunity go by for some good, fun Air Force/Army rivalry. Since he was so close, I drove over for a weekend, to see him and his family.

While I was there, he invited me to do physical training, or "PT," with him. Since I was already going to do it, I said "Sure. Let's go!"

As I laced up my running shoes, Jim dropped a back pack by me. He informed me that we were going for a Ruck March. "Fortunately" for me, he had an extra ruck sack for me.

Knowing that I would never hear the end of it, I was not about to say, "I'm Air Force. We don't do Ruck Marches." I said, "Great! Let's go!"

I strapped on the ruck sack and stood to start down the driveway. Jim said, "You forgot these." I turned and, to my surprise, he reached down and began to put bricks in his and then my ruck sack!

Knowing that I would never hear the end of it, I was not about to say, "I'm Air Force. We don't do Ruck Marches with BRICKS in our rucks!" So I said, "Put an extra one in mine!"

When he finished putting what felt like 97 pounds of bricks in my ruck, we headed out. It did not take long for my body to suggest to me that it was not used to carrying bricks and jogging. After another mile, it strongly suggested it really was not used to it. After another mile, my body flat out told me that it did not like me any more for doing that to it!

Knowing that I would never hear the end of it, I was not about to say, "I'm already worn out and ready to stop, or drop." So I kept jogging.

The weird thing was that, after a while, I just got used to carrying all that weight. I focused on other things and got into a rhythm of jogging. I knew it was still there and still a struggle, but I just kept going.

The miles finally wound down. We turned the corner of the street and his house came into sight. We rounded the end of the driveway and stopped at the garage. I unstrapped the ruck and dropped it to the ground (trying not to look like I was desperate to get it off).

As soon as I took it off of me and set it down, I felt like I could jump twenty feet in the air! I had gotten somewhat used to carrying the weight. While I carried it, much of my energy had to be devoted to just staying upright. When I got rid of it, I felt the relief! Then my energy could be used for other things, like moving forward.

I came to realize that experience is a lot like what unforgiveness does to a person. You may get somewhat used to carrying it. Many people have been carrying unforgiveness for so long, they do not have any idea, and even fear, what it would be like to not carry unforgiveness around. But when you lay the burden of unforgiveness down, you feel the weight come off! You feel the freedom that comes from forgiveness!

In fact, in Matthew 11:28, Jesus called for us, who are weary and burdened, to come to Him and He would give us rest. He told us to swap burdens with Him. He told us to take His yoke and burden that is easy and light and learn from Him, and we would find rest.

Although Jesus was not specifically talking about the burden of unforgiveness in this passage, His words are true for this burden, too. When we choose to "come to Him," "take His yoke," and "learn from Him," we find rest. These words require action on our part. Although, as Omnipotent God, He could force us to accept help, He calls for us to take action toward Him. He does not rip our burdens from us, but takes what we give to Him.

What I struggled with, I have found also hinders many people who have been wronged by someone else from truly forgiving are several mistaken beliefs about what the Bible teaches about forgiveness.

Many people believe that forgiveness means they must forget and pretend the offence did not happen. "Forgive and forget," they say. Others believe that to forgive means to allow the Offender back into close relationship, where he or she may hurt them in the same way again. Still others believe that forgiveness means the Offender gets away with what they did. However, none of these are true.

If you have been wronged, in order to truly forgive, you must remember. You must remember the reality of the offense and the reality of the forgiveness given. Biblical forgiveness means we may remember the offence, but we remember that we transferred the right to collect the Justice debt to God Himself. Biblical forgiveness required me to remember the debt I had owed God and that He forgave me of!

If the Offender has broken trust and harmed the relationship in major and fundamental ways (such as abuse), it is not wise to bring him or her back into close relationship, until Repentance and Genuine Apology have been demonstrated and trust rebuilt to the point that safety is proven. That is reconciliation. Remember that forgiveness and reconciliation are NOT the same thing. You can choose to forgive, but you cannot choose to have reconciliation. That requires the Offender to repent!

The last mistaken belief I had about forgiveness goes to the heart of Christian beliefs. "If I forgive, the Offender will get away with it!" If God is truly God and is Righteous, Holy, and Omnipotent, He cannot allow evil to go unpunished forever. And that is the Truth. No one will get away with anything. Every person who has ever lived will stand before God, "the Judge of all the earth", and give an accounting for their deeds and thoughts. But God is the only one righteous and holy enough to be worthy to stand as Judge. And He will!

Through the variety of hard times I have had, I have also learned that God and His actions often don't make sense, at least not to me. I have earned an Associate's degree, a Bachelor's degree, two Master's degrees and am finishing up a Doctorate degree. Like the wise cartoon character, Yogi Bear, "I'm smarter than the average bear." And yet, in large part because of that education, I've realized that I don't know much or see very much of this life, or the whole universe. But God does.

His ways and His understanding and plan for me and all of His creation are so much bigger than my mind can understand. Thankfully, I don't have to understand how it all works together. I believe I have begun to learn what the Apostle Paul knew: for those who love God, it all does work together and God makes sure of that.

Is there someone that you need to forgive? Will you make the courageous choice to forgive and let God take care of the justice?

You may find a prayer like the one on the next page helpful, or you can just pray the words that are inside of you.

My Prayer of Forgiveness

"Lord Jesus, thank you for caring about how much I've been hurt by (*say Offender's name*). You know the pain I felt when he/she (*list the offense/offenses*). You know what it is like to be betrayed. Right now, I choose to release all that pain to You. Thank you for dying on the cross and extending Your forgiveness to me. As an act of my will, I choose to forgive (*Offender's name*). Right now, I transfer the Justice debt out of my book and into Yours. I refuse all thoughts of revenge. I pray that he/she would repent, but I will leave the work of conviction to your Holy Spirit. May Your Will be done in his/her life. I thank you for giving me Your power to be able to forgive, so that I can be free from the burden of unforgiveness. Please give me the continuing strength to live this decision out daily. I pray all this in Jesus' Name. Amen"§§§

---

§§§ I am indebted to June Hunt and her wonderful work, *Forgiveness: The Freedom to Let Go*, for the basic prayer, which I changed to fit me and become my own prayer.

19

THE SHAME OF COMPARISON

As I struggled to understand my battle with PTSD, one thought came to my mind over and over. I felt much shame when I thought about what I was dealing with and what I thought so many others had to deal with. I have come to know that it is a very common reaction to group traumatic events. "My trauma/experience wasn't as bad as so many others. I shouldn't have a problem with it."

What I did not understand at the time was that it is impossible to completely and accurately compare trauma experiences. I had experienced more than many other people. I had experienced far less than others. But whether I had experienced less than some or more than others was rather irrelevant. Two people, next to each other, experiencing the 'same' events, will each react to a different array of factors, inside and outside themselves. One may have a glass that's not quite as full, or has a greater ability to process events and, thus, the strength to weather the current event with no lasting damage. The other may be full to the brim already. Whatever the case, comparing trauma in order to legitimize or delegitimize one's own reactions is fraught with danger. I came to understand and accept that there were many contributing factors to my reactions. I made my decisions and had responsibility for them. Many of them were very good. Some were just plain bad. Even though I now understand many of the contributing factors, there are still others that I still do not fully understand. However, I made decisions that set my course toward wholeness.

I decided that, whatever the causes, I was going to deal with the reality of where I was. I decided that I would always find people who did things better than me. I was determined not to stay in the midst of despair. I did not want to be defined as a victim, or a failure. I could wallow in my "victimhood" or I could get help to overcome it. Whether or not you are struggling because of your own choices or the choices of other people, you face the same choice. If you are suffering from the effects of trauma or are overwhelmed with stress, you can make that same determination.

I have learned that God's Grace is greater than any sin or mistake I've made. If I could go back ten years and do things over, I would change many things. But I can't. Instead, I can surrender and let the Grace of God take all the bad I've done and the bad done to me and leave only the good. That is the choice I have made. What will you choose?

20

WHAT WILL YOU DO WITH YOUR SCARS?

In writing this book, I have come to know in a new way that God can take our scars and glorify Him. He can take our scars and use them to draw other people to Him. where He can demonstrate His love for them. Our scars do not have to define us. They do not have to be the end. Our scars make us unique and our scars connect us to other people with scars.

Over my career in the military, I have stood over perhaps hundreds of flag-draped caskets of those who have served our country, past and present. Many have died of natural causes. Way too many have been killed on the fields of battle. Others died at their own hands. Although. if Jesus does not return before, I know my body will one day be in a casket. Because of the Grace of God, I did not choose my death. I chose life.

God has taken my experiences and used them to prepare me for the next chapter in my life. Because Terri and I had worked very hard to honor God and each other in our marriage, our marriage relationship with each other grounded us in love and helped us survive the trials. We believe that God does not love us more than He loves everyone else. That is why we believe God called us to start The Center for Mighty Marriages & Families after we left the military. The Center exists to help people have strong relationships with God and each other. We obeyed God and we continue to step out in faith to come alongside individuals, couples and families and see God transform them through counseling, marriage intensives, singles, engaged and marriage enrichment conferences or Christian conciliation through mediation and arbitration of conflicts.

God is still enthroned over creation. He did not surrender it during my tour of duty in Iraq, nor in or after Hurricane Katrina, nor in a crisis center with no shoe strings on my shoes. War and disasters like Katrina are a sad consequence of a fallen world. It rains "on the just and the unjust." All of humanity continues to be affected by this sin filled world. As I have had time to think back over the trials, I have become even more excited for Heaven. There will come a day when there will be no wars, hurricanes, earthquakes, fires, nor floods. There will be no more death, no more tears shed. This earth will be redeemed anew and sin will be definitively dealt with. Until that day, I wait and groan in a world filled with pain and anguish and cry out within me the words John, the Revelator, wrote in Revelation 22:20, "Amen. Come, Lord Jesus."

My story continues. Where will you allow yours to go from here?

I pray that if you don't know the hope of that day to come, you will realize your need of God's help and forgiveness. Resolve your Surrender Paradox. Don't surrender to despair. Surrender to God! Call out to Him in prayer, repent (genuinely apologize), ask for His help and surrender to Him. Seek out a chaplain or pastor, or contact us at our website. Any of us would be honored to help you meet Him.

God will take your broken pieces and give you peace. Will you let Him?

CPSIA information can be obtained at www.ICGtesting.com
Printed in the USA
LVOW13s2120111013

356580LV00001B/2/P